HONORING THE FALLEN

A Father's Story

Chad Cartledge

with Jen Jeffrey Billington

ISBN: 978-1-959369-04-2

Faith Words Publishing

This book is dedicated to the brave heroes who have given it all while serving. We will never forget.

reviews always appreciated

Contents

"These families sacrifice more than we will ever know. If I can bring even a little joy back into their lives... it is worth it all."

~ Zechariah Cartledge

Forward

Where can we find hope if we are hopeless? Who understands our pain when we hurt more than anyone else? What is the point of this life—if the person our entire world revolves around is taken away from us?

As children, we read stories of magic and fantasy, heroes and villains, dragons, and lands of enchantment. Remember your childhood—and even the real heroes in your life. Maybe it was your father, your mother. Perhaps it was a firefighter, a police officer, a teacher. The line between magical fantasy and real life was sometimes a blur in your mind. Remember how your heroes could do no wrong, and no one could ever hurt them? In a child's mind, heroes will never fail and will not fall. We carry this forward as we become parents, reading to our children and sharing the epic tales of heroic deeds. Why do we hold these stories and these heroes so highly in our hearts? The answer is profound, yet so simple.

Without heroes, evil wins. Without heroes, there is little hope for good to prevail, and the darkness may overcome the light. Truly, heroes symbolize hope.

When a police officer or firefighter is killed, a piece of our hearts is destroyed forever. A family is shattered, and their community shares in this pain. A feeling of hopelessness overwhelms us all as we think about the family left behind—those who loved that fallen hero with all their being. And deep inside all of us, a piece of our childhood is lost—because heroes aren't supposed to fall. Heroes are supposed to live forever. The deep sadness the family and the community feel leaves us wondering how we will move forward from this tragedy. Getting lost in the darkness can be easy, closing in on our hearts.

First Responders are lost almost daily in the United States as they bravely and selflessly serve their country and community. These heroes—these defenders—are why the wolves do not prey at liberty on the sheep of this world. These are the heroes who give hope to the hopeless every day. While many will never understand the calling into this line of work, those who wear the badge will tell you — this is a true calling.

I was blessed when I began reading this book, Honoring the Fallen. So many people need direction in life. Their only role models are social media or YouTube sensations. Sometimes, the world is filled with people who have lost respect for the value of human life and decency. As an active-duty police officer, I repeatedly see the worst characteristics of humanity. This is just one of the reasons I have such respect for Zechariah Cartledge. Zechariah, the youth runners, and those involved in the mission of Running 4 Heroes inspire millions daily as they create new hope for the hopeless.

Looking at the Officer Down Memorial Page and seeing all the officers killed in the line of duty, your heart stirs with anger, fear, and a desire to honor their lives through your service. Many officers study how the hero fell, trying to learn better how to survive the battlefield themselves. It is even more disturbing to now be able to watch body camera footage of an officer being killed. It's as if the one watching the video is in the middle of the battle—their heart pounding with adrenaline. At the end of it all, you feel hopeless. That is where God embraced Zechariah with purpose and identity, bringing hope and comfort through the mission of Running 4 Heroes.

As you read this incredible true story of how one small boy who wanted to help began a movement that would change the world, you will see new hope begin to form. These fallen heroes' surviving families and communities now see them live on forever. A funeral and a folded flag symbolize the end of the remembrance of this great nation's fallen protectors. Running 4 Heroes gives us so much hope as we see the leaders of tomorrow running in their honor and memory. The Tribute Hall serves a unique purpose in etching the human side of these heroes into our hearts forever. Out of the destruction and sadness, we see hope for tomorrow and a future for the surviving families. This is how we change the world. This is how we change and give hope for the future of our nation.

Years ago, when a refiner purified gold, they would filter it until they could see their reflection. I believe God refines us so that His reflection may be seen in us—so that we are in His image. While the refining process is not comfortable as we face hardships and tragedy, we are not refined to be comfortable; instead, we are refined to be comforters. God will not waste our pain—He redeems our pain by using it to comfort others.

When Zechariah wanted to begin running to honor fallen heroes, he and his family had no idea what God would do with it. The unwavering determination to honor every fallen police officer and firefighter is a profound quest. And as his popularity has grown, it has taken steadfast faith and sacrifice to trust the vision—and to see the purpose behind this vision to bear incredible fruit in bringing comfort and hope.

As you read through these pages, you will see that the miracle continues. In death, there is life. In hopelessness, there is new hope. Over evil, good prevails. And in the face of the darkness, the blue lights flash bright and brilliant—as Zechariah holds the blue line flag high and proud and rounds another lap to honor our heroes. Heroes live forever.

Jonathan E. Hickory

Jonathan E. Hickory - Police Sergeant, Author, and Motivational Speaker

breakeverychainmovie.com

Acknowledgments

All credit goes to my Lord and Savior, Jesus Christ, for calling my family to do something meaningful.

To Zechariah for his obedience in listening to the call, to my wife and daughter for supporting this effort from the beginning, and to my parents and in-laws for all their efforts to support Zechariah and the mission.

To Jen Billington, co-author of the book, for the many hours she has invested into helping tell our story.

To the many volunteers who have served on our Board of Directors and in other capacities—this mission is a team effort, and I am thankful for those who have been part of the team—and to the incredible Youth Runners who understand the importance of continuing our work.

To all our First Responders and K9s who risk it all every day, to those brave heroes who have given it all and whose memories we seek to preserve and honor, and to the surviving families who have lost so much.

Finally, I thank the hundreds of thousands who have supported my son and this mission—individuals and through their businesses and organizations. Your support has meant the world to me and my family; we are forever grateful for you.

Chapter 1

Divine Calling

"You need to come home—something's not right!" There was panic in my wife's voice. December 5th, 2007, was a day my wife and I will never forget.

Three months before that date, we were two newlyweds who discovered we were expecting our first child. We weren't surprised when we found out. We both wanted to start a family soon after marriage. Weeks after finding out we were expecting, we discovered God was blessing us with a boy. Susan and I were ecstatic and hoping to have a son as our first child.

Our vision for our family was to have a boy first and a daughter second, hoping that big brother would be a protector and friend to his little sister. We couldn't contain our excitement when we discovered that our vision was starting to become a reality, so we shared the news with our family and friends via social media.

For weeks following the big reveal, we began purchasing items for our son, who would be named Conner. We took an immense liking to the Snoopy theme, so we stocked up on all the Snoopy and Peanuts items, from bed sheets to wall decals to bottles and binkies.

We were excited to welcome our baby boy, due in March 2008. I worked for a transportation company and was up early that morning to pick up guests traveling from Disney World to the airport. I was just about to pick up the 16-passenger van when my phone rang. It was Susan.

She urged me to come home right away, thinking she was in labor. She was only 22-23 weeks into the pregnancy. I returned home and rushed Susan to the hospital, where we got the news we did not want to hear - Susan had begun giving birth, and it wasn't looking good. She was checked into a room where she delivered a baby boy within a few minutes. His life was a beating heart that only kept beating briefly before it finally stopped.

Our son, whom we anxiously awaited, was with us for 30 minutes before gaining his wings. My wife and I were devastated.

Despite the sorrow and frustration, we never got mad at God. However, we questioned if our faith (or the lack thereof) played a role in the outcome of what happened that December morning. One month after our son's passing, my wife and I decided to *give our lives to the Lord,* and together, we got baptized at our church.

Saying goodbye to Conner

An Unexpected Gift

To our surprise, a month later, Susan was pregnant again—the *positive* result from this pregnancy test brought on many emotions. Fear was at the top of the list. The loss of Conner was still so fresh and new. We still hadn't even reached Conner's original due date before finding out we were expecting another child. We channeled that fear and prayed, asking God to give us a different outcome this time.

Despite losing a son, our hope remained the same. Susan and I wanted another boy, though this time, our reason was more for *healing*. Our closet was still full of baby boy Snoopy items that we refused to discard because we knew we would have a son one day.

Chapter 2

"It's a Boy!"

When the time came, we had an ultrasound. "It's a boy!"

Because of our faith, we knew we wanted to name our son *Christian*. We shared the news of Christian with the world and requested prayers for a different outcome with this pregnancy. We also sat down, talked with our doctor, and discussed how to prevent Susan from another preterm labor.

The doctor explained how there could have been many factors that led to her early delivery, and it was decided that Susan would get weekly checkups to see how things were going. During her first pregnancy, Susan had an incompetent cervix (where the cervix spreads apart too early). She had a feeling that was why we lost Conner because that does run in her family, but the doctors said it could have been for several different reasons and wanted to monitor her.

Week after week, Susan would visit the doctor, and the news was always positive. Things were going well. Susan and I went to Las Vegas early in the pregnancy and returned with no issues. It looked as if things were going in the right direction.

Holding Onto Hope

During her 21-week checkup, everything looked normal, but during the 22nd week, it was like a switch was flipped. Susan's cervix shrank to a dangerous level, and the doctor was immediately concerned. He had her checked into the hospital. Doctors requested that Susan be transported to a hospital specializing in pregnancy complications and premature infants.

During the ambulance ride, Susan and I began to pray. We weren't sure if our hearts could take this, but it seemed we might relive the same nightmare we had recently experienced. We arrived at the hospital, and a doctor saw Susan right away.

After going through the procedures, we were informed that she was in the early stages of delivery and would likely have the baby within a few days. The doctor started to go into detail about what happens when a child is born at the 22-to-23-week mark, but we asked him *not* to go through it. Susan and I were already aware. We just wanted to get to our room and be alone.

Susan was assigned a room on an upper-level floor of the Winnie Palmer Hospital in Orlando with strict orders to remain on bed rest. They provided her with a bedpan because they anticipated that *any* movements could result in our son's early delivery. Their goal was to keep Christian in Susan's womb as long as possible.

The nurse came in for a routine check and informed Susan she would be given a nightly injection. She explained that the injection was a steroid designed to increase the development of the child's lungs if Susan delivered early. The lungs are one of the last things to develop in a child, and they wanted to give Christian the best opportunity to survive if he was born prematurely. It was around 2 AM that next morning when she received her first injection - a nightly occurrence that would happen at that same time until she delivered.

We expected Susan would deliver the baby before long, so we stayed together each night in the hospital room, praying, listening to music, and enjoying each other's company the best we could. Fortunately, the hospital food wasn't that bad, giving us something to look forward to each night – dinner *together*.

God Remembered

About two weeks into her stay, Susan and I had a supernatural feeling overcome us. It almost sounded like a voice calling us, telling us to read about Zechariah in the Bible. We did. We read about how Zechariah and his wife, Elizabeth, wanted to have children but could not conceive because they were old. They kept faith that they would be blessed with a child one day.

They were blessed with a son named *John the Baptist*. This story was great, but my wife and I weren't sure we understood why *we* were called to it. They had an issue with having children, but their reason was *age*. My wife and I were both in our early 20s, so there was a big difference in our difficulties.

We put the Bible away and resumed our daily routine, which consisted of waiting, waiting, and even more waiting. Several weeks went by, and once again, we were overcome with this feeling that we were missing something about the story of Zechariah.

If it were just me, I likely would have ignored it and moved on, but Susan had the *same* feeling, so we decided to find out what the name Zechariah *meant.*

We did a quick internet search, and the moment we saw the meaning, we were overcome with chills—as if God was speaking directly to us through this name. Zechariah means "God has remembered." At that moment, we felt God reminding us that He had remembered what we had endured and that this pregnancy would be different for us since we kept our faith.

At that moment, we vowed to change our son's name from Christian to Zechariah, but we still wanted to keep our faith as part of his name, so we agreed to give him the name "Zechariah Christian," which translates as *"God has remembered the follower of Christ."*

What should have been a short stay at the Winnie Palmer Hospital turned into an 8-week stay. Susan was there so long that they decided to move us to a different room every two weeks to change our view. We even had prime real estate to watch Hurricane Fay enter the Florida Peninsula. When Susan reached week 32 of the pregnancy, they felt she was far enough along to return home, so she was discharged with orders to remain on strict bed rest while at home.

Welcome Zechariah Christian

Two weeks later, we returned to the Winnie Palmer Hospital when she showed signs of going into labor. When they broke her water, they realized that the reason Susan didn't deliver earlier as she did with Conner was because there was a *double sack* surrounding Zechariah which is not very common. God put a second level of protection to ensure that when the cervix shrunk, the double sack could keep the weight of the baby intact.

On October 21st at 8:16 AM, a four-pound, 10-ounce child was welcomed into the world. This child had the loudest set of lungs we could recall, and despite being very tiny, he had no health issues.

He was so healthy that after two additional nights at the hospital, he was discharged to go home. Zechariah Cartledge was here, and our prayer for a healthy baby boy was answered. Zechariah had an original nickname that didn't stick, but for a while, we called him our "double sack-eriah."

People never really understood it, and we didn't want to go into details, so… we let that one go.

God remembered us. We didn't name our child; *God* named him. Our blessings continued as Susan bore our third child three years later. A beautiful and healthy baby girl named Chloë. Susan remained at high risk for her pregnancy with Chloë but was approved to have the cerclage surgery early to be safe. Susan could remain active throughout the pregnancy with Chloë. We decided that when God granted us our wish of a boy *and* a girl, that was enough for us - our family was complete.

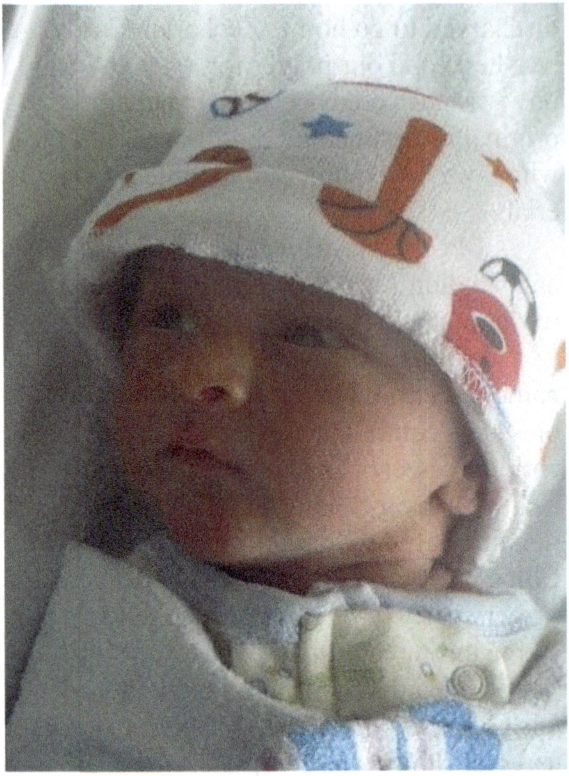

Zechariah Christian Cartledge

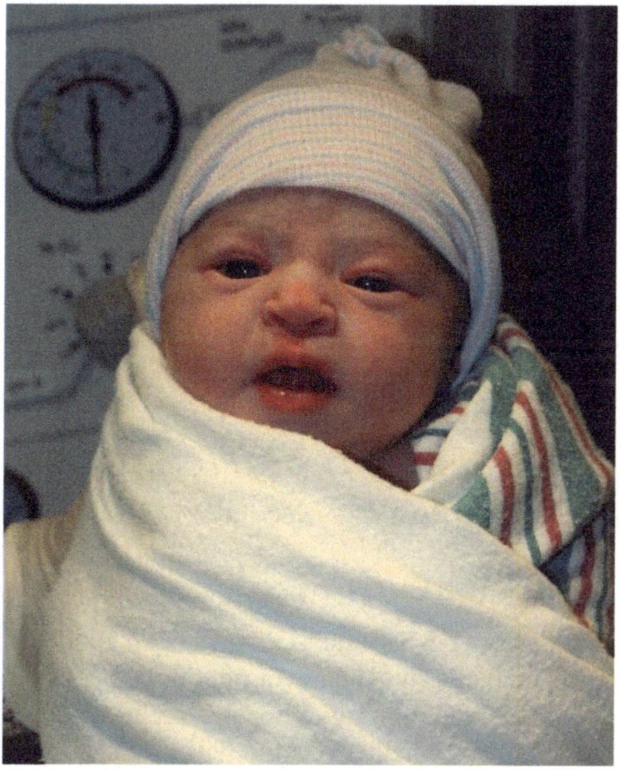

Chloë Gabriella Cartledge

Chapter 3

It Started with a Flyer

Zechariah has always been a kid with much energy. Whatever he did, he needed to move and do it quickly. This included running, whether outside with friends or around the house, driving his parents crazy. Zechariah was attending his Winter Springs, Florida, elementary school when an announcement was made to students offering extracurricular activities.

He heard them mention how cross-country would be starting up, and anyone interested in participating would need to take a flyer home to their parents and have it signed. Zechariah believed cross-country would be something he would enjoy, so he grabbed a flyer and started talking about it after being picked up from school that afternoon. It didn't take long for my wife and me to realize that this would be something he would love, so we signed the paperwork.

Several weeks later, he attended his first cross-country practice. The kids would practice in the mornings twice a week, and the training would last roughly 30-45 minutes before the morning school bell.

During these practices, they learned various stretches, participated in activities, and ran laps around the school bus loop (this would mark the first laps he ever took around this bus loop, which later hosted thousands of miles for fallen First Responders). After many weeks of practicing, the students put their hard work into play.

That year, Zechariah competed in roughly five cross-country events. He would run in the half-mile events with many students across the district who were his age. I will never forget how excited yet nervous he was the first time he lined up at the start/finish line. The horn blew, and the kids raced off down the track. We learned from that first run that Zechariah wasn't a sprinter. Most of the other kids passed Zechariah at the onset, and because the run's distance was so short, he would end the race roughly mid-pack.

This result would be the same week in and week out, and Zechariah's complaint was always the same. He would tell us, "I wish the race were longer. I think I could have passed more people." That didn't deter him from trying his best. He fought hard in each race he ran that year.

Third Grade

When Zechariah began third grade, he remained adamant about continuing with cross-country. He was more excited to run that year because he knew the distance would increase from a half-mile to a full-mile run. He felt that he would do much better with a longer-distance event, and sure enough, he did just that.

In his first *one-mile* run of the year, Zechariah came home with a top 20 finish out of roughly 100 kids in the district, many of whom he competed against the previous year. Zechariah also placed in the top 10 in one event that year. Even still, Zechariah felt he could do even better if he had more time.

Despite showing significant improvements from the prior year, he felt the distance wasn't long enough for him to thrive, and he wanted to try something that would fit his style more. Unfortunately, cross-country in elementary school never exceeded the distance of one mile, so we searched for longer races held in our community.

That evening, we found that a *Luvs-to-Run 5k* was happening in our neighboring city in just a few weeks. A 5k is a 3.1-mile race. We asked Zechariah if he would be interested in trying that event, and he quickly said, "Yes!" So, we signed him up and started prepping him for the race.

Longer Distances

After a few weeks of practicing and getting himself ready, Zechariah was set to take on a new challenge: his first-ever 5k event. I remember how excited he was that morning and determined to give it his all. We arrived at the event, and the environment was welcoming. Music was blaring from the speakers as we approached the bib pickup booth. A kind lady asked for our name before retrieving his bib and handing us the pins to clip the bib onto his shirt. After pinning his number on, Zechariah went to the start/finish line, where he stretched (and, of course, talked to everyone within 10 feet of him.)

Over the next 15-20 minutes, the crowd picked up around him. It was time to start the race. The race emcee gave everyone a few pointers and instructions before providing the runners with their countdown.

5… 4… 3… 2… 1…

And he was off! We could tell right from the start that he was excited and determined. He came running by Susan and me, and we stood there cheering him on; then, he went over and around a corner. At this point, all we could do was wait. Were we nervous? For sure. This was the longest run he had ever done, and even though we knew the course was well-marked and secured, we couldn't tell if anything had happened during the run. Is it possible he tripped and fell? Was he even ready to do a run of this caliber at such a young age? Did he hydrate himself enough and stretch accordingly?

After waiting about twenty minutes, the leading runners began to finish the race. We patiently counted them off but didn't have to wait too long for Zechariah. Several hundred runners participated in this event, but our little eight-year-old runner was about the 20th in line. He looked as strong as ever and came running across the finish line with a look of accomplishment and victory. His first-ever 5k was completed in just over 23 minutes, and his efforts brought a first-place finish in his age group.

We knew then that our son had a gift for running, especially when it came to longer distances, and we vowed to let him participate in these events as long as he continued to enjoy them. After a much-deserved trip to the local ice cream shop, Zechariah quickly inquired about when his next 5k would be. We did some research and saw another 5k was happening not too far from our home just a couple of weeks later. Zechariah excitedly asked us to sign him up, and we did.

Building Relationships

Zechariah became close friends with a kid who lived directly across the street from us. His name was Jorgie. He and Zechariah were very close in age and had many similar interests, especially sports. Many of their days and nights were spent playing basketball and soccer and riding their bikes around the neighborhood.

As it turned out, Jorgie's dad was a police officer who worked for our hometown's police department. His father, officer Jorge, worked a day-shift schedule that got him home around the dinner hour.

After pulling up in his marked patrol unit and parking his vehicle in the driveway, it would be a common practice for officer Jorge to join the boys in a quick pick-up game of basketball. This was a regular occurrence, and we think this constant interaction with a uniformed officer played a big part in Zechariah's childhood. It helped him realize at a young age that our police officers weren't *out to get him.* Like every other hard-working citizen, they want nothing more than to come home safely to their families at the end of their shift.

It just so happened that this officer called "home" the house across the street from us. Call it fate, but it was all part of God's bigger plan.

Chapter 4

Running for a Purpose

We continued to sign Zechariah up for 5ks every other week. He would average two 5ks a month throughout the entire summer of 2017. About three-quarters of the way through that year, in September, we were made aware of a local 5k called the "Tunnel to Towers 5k." We had never heard of the Tunnel to Towers Foundation; it was just another 5k that happened to be on a day that was available for us to let him run.

This particular 5k was originally scheduled a month prior on a date we couldn't make, but due to a hurricane, the run got postponed to a date we *could* attend. We signed Zechariah up like any other 5k, not thinking anything more of it, and the day for *package pick-up* came.

We went to the facility to pick up his race package, and from the moment we walked in, wonderful people greeted us. You could tell right away that the significance of this run was to honor 9/11 fallen heroes. We were automatically intrigued by this type of run.

As we approached the packet pick-up table, we were greeted by two ladies. They suggested that we could get a name badge of one of the fallen first responders who died on 9/11 for an extra five dollars. They encouraged runners to wear the name badge on their shirts during the run. Zechariah wanted to do that.

When they presented him with a badge, Zechariah requested to be given the badge of a fallen police officer. He wanted to honor a police officer because of his best friend's dad. They gave us the name of Officer Walwyn Stuart, one of the 37 Port Authority of New York and New Jersey Police Department (PAPD) officers who died on 9/11. There were 71 officer badges from the NYPD, as well as other fallen officers, and there were 343 badges for fallen firefighters with the FDNY.

When the attacks happened on 9/11, Officer Stuart was patrolling the subway stations down below. Immediately, he helped clear the subway station before running into the towers. Unfortunately, after the towers collapsed, he lost his life. They never recovered his body, but they recovered his badge, gun, and handcuffs, which had his name inscribed on them. After Zechariah got Officer Stuart's badge, he got his race number, and we went home.

The evening before the run, Zechariah took it upon himself to find out more about the 9/11 tragedy because, at his age, he had not yet been exposed to the details or magnitude of 9/11. Instead of explaining it to him, I told him there were very informative documentaries, and I felt he was old enough to see them now—especially knowing he had an appreciation for first responders. I thought it would be good for him to view that.

Zechariah watched documentaries and saw for the first time the images of the planes going into the towers, the towers collapsing, and all the first responders rushing in while everybody else was running out. After that, he wanted to learn more about Walwyn Stuart. He began researching Officer Stuart and Firefighter *Stephen Siller* because the Tunnel to Towers Foundation was made to honor Firefighter Siller.

Siller's story is that on 9/11, he had just completed his shift and was going to play golf with his brothers when he got news of the attacks. He called his brothers and told them he would have to *get a rain check* because something was going on at the World Trade Center (WTC) that he needed to help out with.

Firefighter Siller turned around with his firefighter gear still in the bed of his truck. When he got to the Brooklyn Battery Tunnel, he grabbed all his gear and ran through the tunnel straight to the WTC site, where he would sadly lose his life.

The Tunnel to Towers Foundation began honoring him in their first 5k event in which they ran through the Brooklyn Battery Tunnel to the WTC site, just like Stephen did - an event held annually since 2002. The tunnel is 1.73 miles long, and he came out on the other side, still about a mile away from the WTC site, carrying all his gear. When he arrived, he started rescuing people, but the towers collapsed.

A Game Changer

We went early the following day to the Orlando Tunnel to Towers 5k, and that run was a game changer for Zechariah not only because of how many first responders ran that run with him, but also because they ran in their *full gear*. To see all the police officers and firefighters coming together to do this run to honor the fallen heroes from 9/11 set something off for Zechariah. It inspired him, and he spent all morning getting photos with many first responders (some of whom come to *his* runs even today).

That pivotal moment was when he realized he wanted to keep his running geared toward first responders. He realized he'd been doing 5ks for fun, but now he would be doing them for a purpose. Zechariah finished the run in the top three of his age group. That evening, he wrote a report for school that would tell all he had learned leading up to the run and how it inspired him.

His three-page report impressed me that I recorded a video of him reading it and uploaded it onto social media.

The Kid's Got Something

A day or two later, I received a message from the Clearwater Tunnel to Towers group – they are about two hours away from our home. They were so moved by Zechariah's report that they invited him to read it during the opening ceremony of their 5k event, which would take place a month later. I talked with Zechariah and my wife and ensured our schedule was good. That weekend was open, and we decided to spend it in Clearwater to attend the event and allow Zechariah to get up on stage for the first time and read his report.

The Honor Guard came out during the opening ceremony, presented the colors, and introduced Zechariah. When he walked up on stage, it was the first time that I saw Zechariah get up in front of a crowd to speak. He hadn't done that before, and it wasn't anything he had memorized. Even reading, he was so strong in his delivery that you could tell how much he *believed* in what he was doing.

This nine-year-old kid went up on the stage and shared this story, and my wife and I looked at each other and realized this kid had something special… From there, it blossomed. Zechariah went from running just for fun to running for a *cause.*

We knew Zechariah's delivery could be impactful and make a difference. Hearing this message come from a kid was very inspiring. That was when things started to launch. Zechariah has a way of getting in front of people and captivating them, capturing their hearts.

Zechariah's Written Report from 2017

September 11, 2001, was a day that changed the world. It was on that day when four planes were hijacked with the intent to attack the United States. Two of the four planes were flown into the Twin Towers in New York City, and both buildings collapsed shortly after.

In all, 2,977 people lost their lives that day. One of the people who lost their lives was a firefighter named Stephen Siller. Stephen was a husband and had five children. On the morning of September 11th, Stephen had just finished his shift and was on his way to play golf with his brothers when the attack happened.

Since Stephen loved to help others, he called off the golf game, turned his truck around, and went to help. When he arrived at the tunnel, he found the tunnel to be closed to car traffic. Stephen put on his fire jacket, grabbed his 60 pounds of gear, and ran to the tunnels en route to the towers. He would lose his life shortly after while saving others.

A year after Stephen's death, the Siller family started the Tunnel to Towers Foundation in honor of Stephen. The foundation also honors all firefighters and police officers who sacrificed their lives that day. The first fund-raiser for the foundation was a 5k in New York City. For the 5k, they ran through the same tunnel that Stephen ran through a year before and ultimately retraced his steps.

Fifteen years later, the Tunnel to Towers Foundation continues to run 5ks around the United States. The next Tunnel to Towers 5k is happening today in Clearwater, Florida. I am excited to be participating in the 5k. All of us are running in Stephen Sillers's honor. I am also running to honor the life of Walwyn Stuart.

Walwyn Sturt was a police officer who died on September 11, 2001. Walwyn was born on February 13, 1973. He was the youngest of six children who loved the Lord and played baseball and chess. He had a wife named Thelma and a daughter named Amanda. He worked for the New York Police Department for four years. When his wife was pregnant, he switched police departments and went to the Port Authority Police Department because he wanted something safer. He died while saving others who were trapped in the Twin Towers.

I am so excited for this 5k. I am thrilled to be able to honor the heroes of

September 11th. I hope they will always be remembered.

Chapter 5

A $10,000 Goal

After returning home, Zechariah continued honoring Officer Walwyn Stuart and running to support the Tunnel to Towers Foundation. At the end of the year, he made a goal for himself that in 2018, he would raise at least $10,000 for the Foundation. He also wanted to raise enough money for the New York run 5k. He was compelled to follow in Stephen Siller's footsteps and participate in that 5k event.

In January 2018, he planned to run 5ks every other week at different races nationwide. When he did those runs, he wore Officer Stuart's name badge, hoping that it would prompt people to ask him about the badge, allow him to share the story of Officer Stuart, and communicate his goal to the other runners about the New York event.

He did this throughout spring and summer. It was about June or July when he achieved his goals, raising just over $10,000 for the Foundation while raising enough funds to run in New York and having our family go with him.

Zechariah could specify The Foundation's online fundraising platform as his portal. When he created that link, all his funds went straight to the Foundation through Zechariah's channel. We could share that link on my personal social media page so people could donate.

Our local community also embraced what he was doing. He gave a brief speech on Walwyn Stuart and the Foundation at our local Rotary Club of Winter Springs. Zechariah was also invited to speak at our local Optimist Club.

A few months later, he did his second Tunnel to Towers Orlando run, which took place several weeks before the trip to New York. Since Orlando was where it all started the year before for Zechariah, it was at their run that he handed over the check to the Foundation for around $11,000.00. He not only hit his goal but *surpassed* it, and he won an award that year for being the largest fundraiser out of *everybody*.

I kept track of all his 5ks and logged the times because he was very competitive. He always wanted to know his times and would always do the chip-timed events. He ran 16-20 5ks between January and September that year. It was the best way he could share the story of Officer Stuart and the message of what he was doing and encourage people to support his efforts for the Foundation.

Because of his efforts, Zechariah was acknowledged by his school during the 2018-19 school year. He received the Disney Dreamers and Doer Award, established in 1984 to recognize young people who demonstrate excellence at school, home, and community.

That was an incredible honor because it is one of the most significant awards you can get from your school in any given year. The teachers collectively decide who gets that distinction, and out of his entire elementary school, Zechariah received the award during his fourth-grade year.

Personal Goals

The year 2018 was the first time he ran to raise money. He was *inspired* to run the year prior, but 2018 was the year he realized he could make a *difference* while honoring the fallen.

Zechariah's energy has always been nonstop, so he was pretty determined when he decided this was what he wanted to do. Even though he was running for a cause, he liked the notion of competing and would go out there and run for *time* and personal records. He was still doing cross country at his school and continued wearing the name badges during his cross country meets.

Never once did he walk a 5k. Zechariah always ran the entire race and finished. During that time frame, his best time was 23:57 for a 5k. At every event that Zechariah competed in, his biggest fan was always his little sister Chloë. Whenever Zechariah would finish a 5k, Chloë would run up to him, give him a hug, and show the love she had for her brother. Whenever Zechariah received an award for his time, she would be the loudest one cheering. They also get on each other's nerves at times, but that is to be expected.

Fundraising

Planning for the run in New York, we made specialty shirts to raise funds. These shirts were exclusively to raise money to help get Zechariah to New York City – not the money we were giving back to the Foundation. We did get the Foundation's approval to have their logo on the front of the shirts, and it said *Team Zechariah* underneath.

Under Team Zechariah were the names of four of the first responders he wanted to find on the *National September 11 Memorial Wall* and whom he planned to represent when he did that run. Walwyn

Stuart's name was on the top, followed by Robert Parro, Samantha Lightborn-Allen, and John Talignani.

A cool thing about the shirt was that the names of those who sponsored Zechariah on the back were made into a silhouette of the World Trade Center.

A few side notes: Zechariah is a big NASCAR fan, and his favorite driver has always been Michael McDowell. He became a household name after winning the Daytona 500, but Zechariah was a fan long before his name was synonymous with NASCAR. Zechariah was fortunate to have met Michael McDowell twice when he was younger, and it meant the world to him when McDowell became one of the first people to donate to his fundraiser for the New York run.

Cy Curnin, the lead singer from The Fixx, an 80s rock band from London, also donated. This donation meant the world to my mother, Zechariah's grandmother, because she is a big fan of The Fixx. So much so she calls herself a "fixxture."

Chapter 6

New York, Here We Come!

We were beyond excited. This would be our kids' first visit to New York City, and their enthusiasm was very high the day we flew up.

We would only be there for about a week, and there were a lot of different events, but we also wanted to make sure the kids got to experience New York, taking in a Broadway show or two and taking the subway. However, our first experience in New York started a little *frightening* for me.

I worked full-time as a financial aid compliance manager for a local university, and I hated returning from a trip to catch up on hundreds of emails. So, I made it a habit to take my work computer *with* me, and I would go through work emails in the evenings.

We had flown to New York on JetBlue Airlines (who graciously sponsored the flight) and arrived at the JFK Airport. We had been informed that it would be easiest for us to get around by subway.

When we arrived at the station, we sat on a bench waiting for the train. Everything was good when we got on—the kids were accounted for, the doors closed, and we started moving.

Panic On The Subway

A few moments after the subway departed, I realized my shoulder didn't feel as *heavy* as usual. I looked around and didn't see my laptop bag! I knew I had it when we sat at the subway station and knew immediately that I had left it on the bench. It was my *work* laptop. Not only was it my work laptop, but in the sleeve of thc laptop case were the Broadway tickets to the show we were going to that week.

Ironically enough, I didn't want to leave them in our book bag because I didn't want to leave the book bag accidentally. I was adamant that I would not forget my laptop, but sure enough, I left the laptop.

Unfortunately, it was about four stops before we could catch an exit, allowing us to take a returning subway. It took us 45 minutes to get where we needed to return to the station. We called the New York City Transit Authority and the subway station, but nobody saw anything, and they said they would keep us posted. We arrived at the stop, and I looked where we were sitting - nothing was there. I knew somebody had picked it up, and I panicked.

I asked an officer I saw walking by if he knew if anybody had turned in a laptop – he said no, and the best thing we could do was to talk to the customer service agent at the front of the station. There must have just been a shift change because I asked the lady at the front desk, and she said she had just gotten there and somebody might have dropped off a bag, but she would have to radio in and see.

She went off to the side to talk to somebody in the back. I noticed she left a back door open behind her, and I saw what looked like my laptop in the back room. When she returned, I said, "Ma'am, that bag might be mine." She brought it forward and asked if it was my laptop. It was!

I expressed relief and thanked her. All the tickets were still in there. Another lady working there had seen when it was dropped off and said, "Oh, we were just about to call you and let you know a lady dropped this off and said she saw it by the chair over there."

I had already played the entire reel in my mind – *"How would I tell my boss? What would my company do? It wasn't even my laptop – it was my company laptop.* What *would we do about the Broadway show we had tickets for Chloë to see? The trip was already ruined..."* The day started interestingly, but thankfully, it wasn't ruined.

We boarded the next subway going out and arrived in New York City at the hotel where we were staying. It was right across from One World Trade Center. We were given a room that had a beautiful view of the 9/11 memorial.

Thank An Officer

A friend of mine is from New York, and his brother was still working with the FDNY. When we were walking to our hotel, a few fire trucks were waiting out in front of the hotel to welcome us upon our arrival. Zechariah was able to meet and talk with them, and every time he saw a law enforcement officer or firefighter, he would also make sure to go up to them and tell them, "Thank you."

A moment I won't ever forget is when he walked up to this one officer and said, "Sir, I just want to thank you for what you do." And the officer looked at him and said, "Young man, I have done this job for three years at this same place – this is my station, and in those three years, I have *never* had anyone walk up to me just to say thank you. Usually, they are walking up to me to complain about somebody, or that something is wrong, or walking up to bad-mouth me - you are the *first* person who has ever walked up to say thank you."

He ended up giving Zechariah a patch and a couple of coins. It was then that Zechariah understood that what he was doing was something *remarkable*.

When we checked into the hotel, the first thing we did that day was head straight to the National September 11th Memorial Wall at the fountains, where Zechariah would find Walwyn Stuart's name. When he saw it, he reached out his arm and placed his hand upon that name.

The emotions I felt watching my son's experiences were almost overwhelming, and this was also my first time seeing the memorials. We also found Stephen Siller's name because Zechariah spent the year trying to raise money for the Stephen Siller Tunnel to Towers Foundation.

We also found the name of a fallen firefighter, the relative of one of our friends. They had asked if we could search for his name, so we did. We found his name and sent them a picture.

After finding the names, we spent a few hours walking around the memorial before grabbing dinner and returning to our hotel for the night. That first day was more about just *taking it in*.

Honoring the Fallen – A Father's Story

Chapter 7

New York Part Two

September 30, 2018 – the day of the running event. One notable thing about that particular run was that I ran it with Zechariah. I don't do 5ks, but I knew how special this one was and wanted to do it with him.

The Tunnel to Towers 5k run is in Brooklyn and Manhattan. It starts at the Ikea parking lot on Beard St. in Brooklyn and ends at the corners of West and Murray Streets in Manhattan.

We woke up early that morning and walked over to the ferry, where we said our temporary goodbyes to Susan and Chloë. They walked to the finish line, where they awaited our arrival.

It was a cold morning, but our views of New York City from the ferry were stunning. Seeing the World Trade Center, the Statue of Liberty, and all the different sites just as the sun rose was spectacular. It was a beautiful morning and a beautiful *experience.*

The boat ride took about five minutes, but we had the perfect seat to see the New York skyline fading off in the background as we headed to the other side of the channel.

Zechariah is a very competitive kid, and whenever he runs, his goal is to get as close to a record time as he can, but he knew the significance of this run. In past runs, firefighters would line up for almost a mile as runners exit the tunnel, holding signs with the names of every first responder killed on 9/11.

Many stopped running and would walk to take it in, looking at the photos. Zechariah looked at me on the ferry and said, "Dad, for this particular run, I am not going for *time.* I want to be able to take it in. I want to experience it."

I said, "Absolutely." I also had the usual parental talk with him since he would finish the run well before me to make sure he knew Mommy would be at the finish line. When he got to it, he would know where to find her, and I would meet him there as well. We had that understanding so he would not get lost amongst the thousands.

The Tunnel to Towers 5k brings out thousands upon thousands of people retracing the steps of firefighter Stephen Siller. It's a big event, and many organizations will create and operate teams. We were asked to meet with this law enforcement group called *Brothers Before Others*, who were doing the run. They asked Zechariah to run with their contingency of officers. Each year, that group honors a specific fallen officer from that region, and this year, they were honoring Sgt. Michael Chesna, from the Weymouth Police Department of Massachusetts. Officer Chesna died on July 15, 2018. His wife ran that run as well.

Zechariah was the guest of honor for this group. They gave Zechariah a unique blue-line flag and asked him to carry it in honor of Sgt. Chesna. They made two flags for this run, and his wife had the other flag. Zechariah agreed to take the Chesna flag for the duration of that run. They presented him with the flag and his pole, and we got lined up, and the run started.

As the run was happening, I was getting messages from my dad in Florida as they were live-streaming the run on one of the national news outlets.

He watched as the first crowd started running, but because we were a little farther back, it took about 20 minutes for our group to start moving. My dad kept asking where we were and how he could see us. I told him, "Dad, you won't be able to see us. There are way too many people down here." We did the run, and from my perspective – it was compelling.

Hundreds of first responders ran in their full gear—some ran with tanks on their backs. Every age you can imagine was there. When you run out of the tunnel and see police officers and firefighters holding large signs with pictures of every fallen officer and firefighter, it is pretty powerful.

Even though Zechariah was carrying Sgt. Chesna's flag and was part of that group, he still wore Officer Walwyn Stuart's name badge and his tee shirt with Officer Stuart's name and the three others he honored for the run. In his mind and heart, he was still doing that run to remember

Officer Walwyn Stuart but would also use it to honor other fallen heroes.

It took me about an hour or so, and I didn't have a chip on my bib, so I never saw my official time, but being the kid that Zechariah is, even though he took his time on this run, he still wanted to know what his time was. So we paid a little more to have his time as a *chip time*. He finished the run, and this was one of the first moments of his mission when we realized it was a *God-thing*.

When they first posted the runners' times, they didn't have the tenth of a second listed. They only had the hour, minutes, and seconds, so they rounded up at the first call of the results. They added the tenth of the second when they posted the official results.

When they first called the times, Zechariah's time was 37.28. Somebody contacted us right away when they saw his time and realized its significance. We had spent all year honoring the Port Authorities' fallen officer, and they knew we were there honoring him in this run.

Thirty-seven officers from the PAPD died on 9/11, and the Port Authority officer who first saw Zechariah finished in 37 minutes said, "Zechariah came here to run for one of our own and finished in 37 minutes - that is one minute for every one of our officers". But then he was even more amazed because the seconds Zechariah finished was called at *28 seconds* – Walwyn Stuart was 28 years old when he passed away on 9/11.

Wait, what? No way. How do you *do* that? It just doesn't happen. *Nothing* is a coincidence with God. It was one of the biggest eye-openers that God had His hand on this as we saw little signs that reminded us of what was happening. To know that his time for this run is history – a minute for every Port Authority officer and a second for every year Walwyn Stuart lived. It's incredible. Several hours after the run concluded, the official timer to the tenth of a second was posted, and his official time was 37:27.9. And at my request, my time remained unlisted (but we know it would have been over an hour).

Stephen Siller
Tunnel to Towers Foundation
TEAM ZECHARIAH
Honoring:
9427

Thelma

After the run, our family stayed for the ceremony and heard from Frank Siller, the CEO of the Tunnel to Towers Foundation; Zechariah got to shake his hand. After the ceremony, somebody from the New York Post pulled us aside and said, "We heard about your son, and we want to do a story on him." We agreed.

So they pulled Zechariah aside, and we went into one of the buildings near the World Trade Center so they could interview him and make it a little quieter. They ended up interviewing him for 30-40 minutes, and the article would be published two days later. Following the interview, we spent the rest of the evening socializing with first responders and taking in the beauty of New York City. We closed the evening by enjoying a beautiful ferry boat ride down the Hudson. Susan and Chloe were able to experience some of that same beauty Zechariah and I experienced that morning.

The article about Zechariah was published the day before we were headed to fly out, and one of my favorite pictures of Zechariah is of him holding one of the newspapers we bought right there in New York City. It was surreal to go up to a newspaper stand in New York City and see a story about our son. We just thought it was fantastic. Needless to say, we bought several copies of the newspaper. The rest of that day was just a fun leisure day, and we watched Phantom of the Opera that night.

One of the things we planned to do before we left was to meet with Walwyn Stuart's widow.

Her name is Thelma. She couldn't come to the run; I don't remember the exact reason (returning to that area is always difficult for survivors). The PAPD was able to coordinate an opportunity to meet her the day that we were to leave. When I told the people who interviewed Zechariah that we would meet with Officer Stuart's widow they asked us to follow up with them after we met her because they might want to do a story regarding that meeting.

Tuesday, October 2nd, was the day we were to fly home and the day we were to meet Thelma. So, members of the PAPD reached out to us and asked us for the time of our departure. We told them our flight time and that we would go through the subway station. They said, "When you get off the tram at the JFK stop, there are going to be three uniformed officers waiting for you. Follow them." I thought, "All right, let's do it."

We packed our bags, got on the subway, and arrived two hours before boarding our flight (as the PAPD requested). We got to the JFK subway station, and as the doors opened, multiple officers were waiting for us, just as they indicated.

We grabbed our luggage and followed them to the platform, where we got into patrol cars. They put me in one car and Susan and the kids in another, and we headed toward the airport. We went around a back entrance that brings you to the Jetway of the tarmac – or, as Zechariah would quickly say, "There's no such thing as a Tarmac; it's a Taxiway." We go through this *every* time.

One of the surprises they planned was to show how close they could get to the airplanes as they were taking off—something incredible to watch.

A whole line of planes were about to take off, so they brought us onto a back road parallel to the runway.

When a plane began moving, the police car just gunned it and bolted down the road! We got to race a jet, and as it took off, we beat it! At the end of the runway, they pulled to the side of the road and let us watch the planes.

After about fifteen minutes, they drove us back to the station and took Zechariah and Chloë out on their firetruck – Thelma wasn't there yet, so we had time to burn. The PAPD at JFK is both a police and fire station. They took Zechariah and Chloë out on the water truck to distract them. Susan and I stayed behind, and that is when they brought Thelma out. Susan and I got to meet Thelma for a bit – Zechariah had no idea that Thelma would be there.

When they pulled up in the firetruck, Zechariah got out, and Thelma was waiting. When he saw her, he came up and gave her one of the longest hugs that I'd ever seen him give. Meeting her was just so emotional and incredibly moving. The press wrote an article on Zechariah meeting Thelma, the wife of this fallen officer he'd spent all year honoring.

The article reads:

"I'm really happy to meet you," said Zechariah, who flew up from Winter Springs, Fla., for the annual run. "I've been waiting to see you for so long." Zechariah, wearing a photo pinned to his shirt and a camouflaged PAPD baseball cap, was greeted warmly by Stuart as his dad shot a

video of their meeting. "You are honoring that man – my hubby," said Thelma Stuart, pointing at the photo on the boy's chest. Thank you so much. Of all the many thousands of officers, you chose mine."

Walwyn Stuart, 28, helped evacuate the PATH station at the World Trade Center before joining the rescue effort in the north tower before his death in the Sept. 11th, 2001 rescue effort. Zechariah gave the widow a letter praising her husband's heroism. The two spent about 45 minutes together before the family returned home.

The young runner learned of Stuart at the Tunnel to Towers race last year in Florida. Each runner got a badge bearing the name of a first responder. Zechariah got handed one for PAPD officer Walwyn Stuart, his dad said. "Once he got the badge, and we got home, the first thing he wanted to do was find out who (Stuart) was," said Chad Cartledge. "He researched and wrote a six-page essay on Stuart, Stephen Siller, and what happened on 9/11." Determined to race this year in New York, Zechariah and his family started fund-raising, and when their goal was met, he told his dad he still wanted to raise money to bring a donation with him for the Tunnel to Towers Foundation.

He handed over $11,000, his father said. The Port Authority contingent let Zechariah lead their group in the race and carry their flag. His dad said Zechariah normally finishes a 5k race in 22-25 minutes- but he told his parents that on this race, he would take his time and absorb the experience. "We expected him to finish a little slower, but when I saw the final time... well, that was very meaningful for me. He came in at 37 minutes and 28 seconds exactly. That would be one minute for every Port Authority cop who died and one second for every year Walwyn Stuart was alive," Cartledge said. Zechariah's next race will be in November in Florida. He'll again wear Walwyn Stuart's badge and another for fallen Firefighter Robert Parro from Engine 8.

A Heart for Survivors

On our flight home, Zechariah and I were talking. What he said next is one of the things that will always stand out, "Dad, why was she so excited to see me?" Zechariah was only nine years old - still very innocent. I said, "Well, because you spent the entire year making sure the memory of her husband stayed alive, and that gesture gave her hope, knowing her husband is not going to be forgotten." After that, he looked at me and said, "Well, I want to do that for other first responders. I want to be able to make other people smile, too."

That statement, I believe, was when the screws started turning in Zechariah's head, and meeting a surviving widow for the first time would set him on the course he's on today. We remain very close friends with Thelma. We talk to her regularly; she is like family, and we love her.

Meeting Thelma Stuart

Photo by American Police Beat Magazine

Chapter 8

The 148

For the rest of 2018, Zechariah continued the mission he set out to do at the beginning of the year, running various 5ks and a half marathon while wearing Officer Stuart's name badge. As we approached the end of 2018, Zechariah noticed that, according to the Officer Down Memorial Page (ODMP), we had lost 148 officers at that point. We use the ODMP to determine when an officer is killed in the line of duty.

An Admirable Goal

We kept a log of every 5k Zechariah did and noticed when we did the math that if we counted every individual mile he ran throughout the year and all those 5ks in 2018, he had run a little over 150 miles.

Going forward, Zechariah's initial idea was to continue running the same 5ks he ran before, raise money for the foundation, and specifically, dedicate each mile to honor one of the first responders killed in the previous year.

For these miles, Zechariah would create a name tag for every first responder who was killed, including their rank, name, department, and the date of their end of watch. He would wear the name tag on his shirt the day he honored them.

Since a 5k is 3.1 miles, he would count that as three miles for three first responders and have three name tags on his shirt. He would announce when he would honor them and share the back story of those officers before the run.

Zechariah wanted to keep everybody updated with these runs, which is when creating a social media page was birthed. He wanted to show people his updates, keep up with his fundraising efforts, and allow people to learn who these first responders were.

A Dad's Support

I took it upon myself during Christmas break to observe what other folks do to share their efforts, and we found this young girl we started following who did honor runs just like Zechariah does, but hers were for *cancer awareness*. She would raise money for what was called *Joy Jars*. They would send jars full of small toys and treats to kids in the hospital who were battling cancer. Her page was called Running for Joy. We got to be friends with her and her family. As we were trying to think of a good idea for Zechariah, I thought, well, Zechariah is running for first responders, and they are *heroes*, so I looked to see if *Running 4 Heroes* was available. Nobody had the user name Running 4 Heroes.

Initially, the Running 4 Heroes Facebook page was designed to keep people up to date with Zechariah's 5ks throughout 2019 and help him raise funds for the Tunnel to Towers Foundation. So, he created his first-ever video for the page. The video was an announcement about his plans for 2019. This was the early start of what would become Running 4 Heroes.

Thinking Small

As part of that initial video, Zechariah informed his viewers that he would be making future clips to show who these fallen heroes were. Before each 5k, he planned to do videos introducing everybody to his mission and telling them about the person he was honoring. The videos were shared directly on the Running 4 Heroes page prior to the runs.

Zechariah planned to do these video clips for all first responders who had been killed in 2018, and *that* was his mission.

Regarding the fundraising goals, Zechariah announced that he wanted to raise $100 for the Tunnel to Towers Foundation for every one of the 148 officers killed in 2018. At the end of 2019, he wanted to be able to hand a check to the Tunnel to Towers run in Orlando for at least $15,000.

Officer Thomas Coulter of the Daytona Beach Police Department in Florida was scheduled to be Zechariah's first mile on the Running 4 Heroes Facebook page. That mile was to be conducted as part of the *Beachin It 5k,* taking place in early

February on the shores of Daytona Beach. Zechariah wanted his first mile to be conducted in the city where one of our local officers served and was lost in the prior year. These plans were made in early January 2019.

Then, Zechariah caught a moving story on the evening news that would change *everything*.

Chapter 9

Girl in the Blue Dress

On January 10th, Zechariah heard a newscast on the television talking about Officer Natalie Corona of the Davis Police Department in California, who had just died in the line of duty. That news clip changed the scope of the Running 4 Heroes' vision and focus. The news story of Natalie showed a picture of her in her blue dress, holding the blue line flag. Zechariah looked at me and said, "I'm running for her, too, right?" I told him, "If you were to run for her, it wouldn't be until next year because she was killed yesterday." He said, "But I don't want her family to wait." I told him he had already committed himself to over 150 miles doing the 5ks, and there weren't any more 5ks for him to run.

It was his idea to add these one-mile runs because every night, he would run the loop around our neighborhood just for fun. He asked, "What if instead of doing practice or training miles, I just do a mile for her and anyone else we lose *this* year, too?"

I didn't see how it was possible. I said, "But Zechariah, if we lost 148 officers last year and try to add on this year's fallen officers, you will add another 148 or so miles this year." He said, "I don't mind. I think we should do something because I don't want them to be forgotten."

So I asked how he wanted to do this. He said, "We can do it right outside, but I want it to be different. Instead of what I do with the name tags for the 5ks I run, what if I carry a flag like I did in New York for Officer Chesna?" I agreed, and we went outside to let him run.

As we were about to start the run, Zechariah said, "Dad, you need to record it. We have the Facebook page now, so if you post it, the family might see it and get some comfort." His first run for the page was completely unscripted, and we were winging it – I didn't know how it would go, and this would be live on Facebook. Zechariah told me that 4 ½ times around the loop was a mile and told me where I could stand to record him.

When I began recording, Zechariah provided facts and details about Officer Corona. What impressed me most was that he had insisted on saying a prayer before the run from the very first mile. He told everyone he would take a moment to pray silently.

Once he started running, he went around, and I thought there was *a lot of dead space there* because he was on the other side of the neighborhood, and nobody could see him. So, I started reminding people of what happened to Officer Corona throughout Zechariah's run.

These first videos were not recorded and uploaded later—we were doing them live. Zechariah wanted families to be able to watch them as they were happening. The incredible thing about doing them live is that I had a 10-year-old kid doing this, and I had to have faith that he would say the right things and not forget details—it was either going to be powerful or "cute but doesn't hit the mark" for his mission.

The run went crazy-viral! Once he completed the run, Zechariah felt so good about what he just did. "He told me, "We had two more that have already passed away this year, so I want to make sure to do their mile, too." So he went back to do the other two runs for those officers, setting off the *one-mile tribute runs*. We weren't sending flags to families yet, so the only Blue Line Flag we had was the Chesna flag he was given in New York City. That flag already had much sentimental value for him.

He did the first few runs carrying that flag. It now hangs in the Memorial Hall beside Natalie Corona's picture and uniform. At the time of her passing, she was 22 years old and had just started her law enforcement career six months earlier.

This was her dream career. She was on the scene of a three-vehicle crash, and somebody not even related to the crash, riding a bicycle, pulled out a gun and started randomly shooting at the first responders and killing Officer Natalie Corona.

Her story moved Zechariah so much that he completely veered off course with his initial plans. What is incredible is that he still kept the promise to the families of the fallen who had died in 2018. He still did every one of those 5ks and half-marathons that year, and they had added 15 more names for 2018. Zechariah ended up running 357 miles by the end of 2019.

Because Officer Corona's death moved Zechariah, he felt guilty about only running for the prior year's officers while the families of the current year were mourning the deaths of their officers, and he wanted to make sure they got their run, too.

January 12th, 2019, was the night he did the run for Officer Natalie Corona. That officially became his first mile under the Running 4 Heroes banner, but again, we weren't an organization; this was just the name of his page.

Zechariah did other things throughout the year to stay relevant and would do what he called *Hero's Hero* interviews. He would interview some of our local officers to ensure his page had wholesome content. In those early interviews, seeing Zechariah as a kid resonated with people. He got to ask uniformed officers about their favorite flavor of ice cream, hobbies, and different questions that made people see the officers' personalities and genuineness.

He started the first one-mile run video by reminding people of his goals to honor the fallen of 2018 and remember the ones we lost this year. At that time, the fundraising efforts were still the same. He was raising money for the Tunnel to Towers Foundation, bringing awareness to their efforts, and doing it as his overall goal to help the Foundation.

At this point, my perspective was to support Zechariah. My goal in all of this was to be a supportive dad. If he wanted to do this in his free time, it was much better than what some other kids did. I was supportive, but I'll admit that I was like many people, thinking after about a month, he would realize that he bit off more than he could chew and go back to the 5ks. I was pretty confident that the aspect of the additional one-mile runs was too much, and he would end up stepping back from it.

My assumption was wrong. Not only did he continue, but it changed our entire lives. Zechariah, at that age, was still an average kid because he would still get in trouble doing the stupidest things and sometimes lie about it—he was still a kid, but over the next month, things changed my view.

These *things* were both big turning points for me in shaping what would become the Running 4 Heroes non-profit.

Natalie Corona, EOW – January 10, 2019

Photo Credit: Richard Lau

Chapter 10

The Flag Mission

When Zechariah did his first few miles, he ran with the flag he received in New York during the Tunnel 2 Tower run for Sgt. Chesna.

On February 19th of that year, the Florida Highway Patrol lost a Lieutenant named Daniel Hinton. Shortly after participating in Defensive Tactics Training, he suffered a heart attack and passed away. He was added to the ODMP shortly after his passing. We had a few generous folks who had sent us a flag or two by the time Zechariah ran for Lieutenant Hinton; he already had a few Blue Line Flags, each with different designs, and would rotate those flags out. He had stopped using the flag that had Sgt. Chesna's name because he didn't want anything to happen to that flag, so we retired it.

Zechariah did the run for Lieutenant Hinton, and we shared it on the Facebook page. The following day, I received a message from Lieutenant Hinton's son. Hinton had left behind a wife, adult children, and grandchildren. In the message, the son said, "The run meant so much to my mom; I wonder what it would take for us to get the flag Zechariah carried so we can give it to her."

I responded by saying, "We use two or three different flags, and your mom needs this. We want to be sure she gets it. We are happy to send you the flag that he carried."

The son wanted to send something for it, but this was something we wanted to do, and that's where that flag needed to go. Zechariah wanted to write a note when we sent that flag to Lieutenant Hinton's family, so we packed the flag and the message and sent them off.

Zechariah continued with the mission the same way he was doing it. We had two other flags we kept in rotation, and it was not a thought that this would be something we would do all the time with the flags. A few days after Lieutenant Hinton's funeral service, I received another message from the son, and he attached a video clip. It was a private funeral ceremony, and the video was taken from the front row next to his mom.

I watched the Honor Guard walk in carrying an open flag. They walked in front of Mrs. Hinton, folded this Blue Line Flag into a perfect triangle, and placed it on Lieutenant Hinton's chest. After the service, the Honor Guard returned, retrieved the flag, and presented it to the wife. He informed us that it was the flag that Zechariah carried during his run. There wasn't a dry eye.

Susan and I debated whether to show Zechariah the video because it was a pretty emotional visual, but we wanted him to see how much that run meant. I never posted that video because it was private, but I showed it to two or three people close to us; one was a local business owner, and once he saw the video, he said, "We need to do this for *all* of them."

I told him, "The flag costs about eight bucks, with added shipping and the cost of getting it to the family; we are talking at least twenty or so dollars per flag, and that will add up if this is something that we do."

We didn't have a large income - we weren't poor, but with how many miles Zechariah was doing, at 20 dollars a flag (and there were 300 of them), I knew we wouldn't be able to afford that. The gentleman said, "I will fund the first ten. Put it out there - a feeler on your Facebook page, and I bet you people will *want* to be a part of it."

The only time I ever wanted to ask for funds was to raise funds for the Tunnel to Towers organization. I had a bit of discomfort asking people for money for something that wasn't a non-profit; to tell people what we wanted to do as a brand new mission, *would they trust us*?

I had talked with enough people that my concerns were relieved, and I felt this was something we needed to do. I posted a video on Facebook, letting people know what happened and whether anyone was interested in sponsoring a flag for roughly $25 dollars.

I told people that giving would not be tax deductible because we were not a 501(c)(3) nonprofit.

Within 24 hours of that post, we were given enough money to fund the following 150 flags! That was just under $4,000 raised within 24 hours of that post.

We had to tell people to *stop sending money* because we had already raised the needed amount. Having extra money in our account made me uncomfortable, so I immediately moved it to a separate savings account. I didn't like having money that was not mine. This inspired us to discuss becoming our own nonprofit.

The run for Lieutenant Hinton was done on Feb 20th, and between that day and March 6th, we raised enough funds to start sending the flags. On March 6th, 2019, Zechariah did a run for Officer Nathan Heidelberg of the Midland Police Department in Texas. He was killed on March 5th from gunfire - shot and killed in the line of duty. His run was the first run in which the *flag mission* was established.

From there, we sent the flag to the family for every mile that was ever done. We later went to Midland, Texas, in early 2021 to present a grant to an officer, and the family of Officer Heidelberg wanted to meet Zechariah. When we met with them, they showed Zechariah the flag and note that he'd written, and they wanted him to sign the flag. It was pretty special knowing that two years later, this was the same flag that we first sent as a mission, and we could see how much it meant to the family. What was also interesting was seeing over two years how much worse Zechariah's handwriting had become!

His early notes had the neatest handwriting (but I don't fault him when he writes as many notes as he does). He has a strong understanding of what these notes mean to the families. When you think about it, every time a soldier gets killed, the families are sent a letter from the President. He doesn't personally handwrite every note – Zechariah does.

A National Interview

Around February or March, the Tunnel to Towers Foundation was about to pay off the mortgage for a fallen Kissimmee Police officer, Matthew Baxter. Officer Baxter was an officer from a city just miles away from Zechariah's hometown. He was killed by gunfire on August 18, 2017. They would present his family with the paid-off mortgage at an organized dinner event. The Siller Family contacted us before that dinner and asked if Zechariah and I wanted to be a part of that. They wanted him to get a close-up view of what the money he was raising would do.

We went, and while we were having dinner, Frank Siller pulled us aside and mentioned that *Fox & Friends* show was going to interview the Foundation, and he was considering having Zechariah be a part of it. I heard him ask my ten-year-old son, "Would you be comfortable conducting this interview yourself?" Zechariah responded, "Yeah, that would be cool!" but in the back of *my* mind, I was thinking, "Wait, hold up… you're asking my son to go on Fox & Friends in a live interview?"

This is not prerecorded – millions of people watch *Fox & Friends* in the morning;

all I think is, "What if he freezes up? He's on live television – what if he gets quiet and doesn't know what to say?" But Zechariah was adamant, "I *want* to do it." The interview was to take place the next morning in downtown Orlando at 7 a.m.

Zechariah wanted to have reached his goal of raising $15,000 for Tunnel to Towers before the run in Orlando later that year. By this time, we had already raised about $7,200 for that effort. He appeared on Fox & Friends, and they gave him 4 minutes for the interview—not like 20 seconds to say a few words. They *talked* to him and gave him a full-blown segment.

I was a nervous wreck behind the camera, but Zechariah was cool, calm, and collected. If you watch the interview, remember that he was a ten-year-old child. Think about what you would expect from a ten-year-old. Yet, his ability to get in front of audiences and speak was remarkable. Zechariah went into the interview saying he wanted to discuss the *Tunnel to Towers' smart homes* project and the fund-raising aspect. He could tell when they were trying to close the interview before he could get to that, and he just went off and took control to get his words in. You can almost read the mind of Steve Doocy.

For Zechariah to be able to do that at such a young age, we had this vision that this might become something big. This journey might have begun with us thinking it would be powerful to see our kid doing something so special, and it meant a lot, but to see him get in front of a national audience like that and hold himself so professionally, it just struck a different chord.

After the interview, it took about 30 minutes to get home, and from the time of the interview to when we got home, we saw that he had raised a little over $25,000 for Tunnel to Towers.

It was at that moment that we realized Zechariah is not just a talented runner; this kid can get in front of millions of people and give interviews that some adults can't even do! By the end of that day, Zechariah's following on the Running 4 Heroes Facebook page increased from 10,000 to over 50,000!

The creation of the flag mission, coupled with his first national interview, gave Zechariah national exposure and began to change the mission he was on.

Zechariah's one-mile memorial runs first took place in his neighborhood. Soon, local officers caught wind of what he was doing and came to support him as he honored the fallen. As the miles grew, more and more officers came out. It got to the point that whenever Zechariah ran around the block, those living in our circle had a hard time getting in and out during the run. A couple of neighbors didn't care for the sirens either, so we talked with our local police chief and school board about finding another location where Zechariah could do these runs without causing any hindrance for residents or passersby.

Zechariah's elementary school, Layer Elementary, has a bus loop. The same loop Zechariah's Cross Country team would meet for practice.

The school is off a back road on a hill. You can't even see the cars passing by—what a perfect location this would be.

We worked with the school board and the police chief and transitioned on April 19th, 2019, to running at the school. This wasn't meant to be a cute kid running; this was a *memorial* service, and we knew there was a specific way to honor each hero. That is how we view these runs. Zechariah felt it was his *responsibility* to honor these fallen heroes.

Fox & Friends Interview with Steve Doocy

Back the Blue Award

Shortly after Zechariah's interview with *Fox & Friends*, newly elected Florida Attorney General Ashley Moody got wind of the story and was very moved by what she heard.

One of the first initiatives she had as Attorney General was to launch the *Back the Blue Award* campaign, which, per www.myfloridalegal.com, states:

Attorney General Ashley Moody's Back the Blue campaign highlights law enforcement officers, citizens, and organizations taking extraordinary steps to forge positive relationships between law enforcement and their communities. Supporting law enforcement is a top priority for Attorney General Moody, and the mission of Back the Blue is to commend Florida's brave law enforcement and Floridians who back them.

"Florida law enforcement officers risk their lives daily to protect us, and, as Florida's Top Cop, I want to make sure they know we have their backs. The Back the Blue Award is just one way our office will promote the great work of the men and women

who wear the badge and the outstanding Floridians who support them."

-Ashley Moody, Florida Attorney General

We were contacted and told that she had selected Zechariah as the first-ever Back the Blue Award recipient. We were invited to Tallahassee for Zechariah to receive this award.

The family and I drove up and stayed the night in Tallahassee. The following morning, Zechariah received the award at the cabinet meeting with the Attorney General and Governor Ron DeSantis.

That was a significant achievement for Zechariah. Just over a month after he started this mission, his state leaders already recognized what he was doing.

I will share something hilarious: a Tallahassee Newspaper captured images and wrote a write-up on the Back the Blue Award presentation. The article was published on March 2nd, three days after the award.

On the front page of the paper is a photo of Zechariah standing with Attorney

General Ashley Moody and Governor Ron DeSantis with the caption:

"Zechariah Cartledge stands with his parents after being recognized during Tuesday's cabinet meeting."

At this writing, it is still captioned that way online. They were a new Governor and Attorney General, and even a local newspaper didn't recognize who they were. It makes me laugh.

This was an update two years later from the Attorney General's website.

TALLAHASSEE, Fla.—Attorney General Ashley Moody recognizes the second anniversary of the Back the Blue campaign. The Back, the Blue Award is presented to law enforcement officials, individuals, or organizations who have either gone above and beyond the call of duty, shown extraordinary support of law enforcement or made significant inroads in building positive relationships between law enforcement and the local community. Since the award program's inception, Back the Blue Awards have been given to more than 30 police officers, sheriff's deputies, highway patrol officers, police K-9s, private citizens, and community organizations.

Attorney General Ashley Moody said, "Florida law enforcement officers risk their lives daily to protect us, and as the wife of a law enforcement officer, I have witnessed personally the sacrifice and courage necessary to keep that commitment. That is why I created the Back the Blue campaign—to highlight law enforcement officers, citizens, and organizations taking extraordinary steps to forge positive relationships between law enforcement and their communities. I am grateful for each recipient's contributions to building a Stronger, Safer Florida."

The inaugural Back the Blue Award was presented in February of 2019 to Zechariah Cartledge, a then-10-year-old boy from Winter Springs who supports law enforcement by running one mile to honor every fallen law enforcement officer. Attorney General Moody has issued awards to law enforcement officers, community groups, and even police K-9s.

Zechariah is in the history books as our state's first-ever Back the Blue Award recipient.

The Squirrel Story

Sometimes, Zechariah will tell little white lies to avoid trouble – things like taking the last soda from the fridge and saying he didn't do it - but God reminds him that the truth always comes out. When he was about eight, we made him a sandwich he didn't want to eat. Even if we've made something he didn't hate, if it wasn't what he wanted, he acted like it was the worst thing in the world (like a typical eight-year-old).

Susan and I have learned our kids' tricks. When Zechariah didn't want something, he would wait until we weren't watching, dump it in the trash, and put his plate back on the table so it looked like he was done eating. We realized he did this, and we would check the trash can.

So, we made him a sandwich, and not even four minutes later, he said, "I'm done, Dad." We checked the trash because he had complained about having to eat the sandwich, but we didn't see anything. I said, "Zechariah, with all the complaining you just did and how slow you eat when you don't want to eat something, there is no way you are done."

He insisted that he had eaten it and said we could check the trash and look and wouldn't find it. So we did. We checked all the trash cans and looked in the usual places - even behind the refrigerator (and let's not go into the time we found chicken nuggets stuffed under the oven), but we found no evidence that he was lying.

So we let him play his video games. About thirty minutes later, I needed to do something in the front yard. The moment I opened the front door, a squirrel ran by dragging his sandwich!

I hollered, "Zechariah, come here…" The squirrel was already gone but dropped the sandwich. Zechariah came to me, and I said, "So that sandwich you ate was pretty good, huh?" I was standing by the door, so he probably thought, "Oh no…." He had taken the sandwich and thrown it in the bushes, thinking we'd never know, but a squirrel found it and was carrying it on the sidewalk! It was hilarious.

People see him doing things to change the world, but if only they could see his table etiquette…

Chapter 11

Defining the Mission

The following spring, I got a message from a group called "Peacekeepers Inc." based out of Springfield, Illinois. They reached out because they wanted Zechariah to be the grand marshall for an event.

Each year, they do a memorial ride throughout southern Illinois, consisting of motorcycles and Jeeps. Before the ride, they have a ceremony, and they wanted to pay tribute to Zechariah for his efforts in honoring our fallen heroes. 2019 was a rough year for Illinois, and there were many first responders that Zechariah had honored in a run.

Our family talked about it, and this was the first time an organization reached out to ask us to take part in an event. I didn't know how it might work; we didn't have funds raised for mission trips or taking part in events. After raising funds for the flags, we aimed to save up to become a 501(c)(3). However, they wanted to sponsor the trip for the whole family.

The day we arrived in Springfield, law enforcement officers were waiting to escort us to the hotel. They also provided a Jeep so we could participate in the ride. One of the first things they did was take us to the law enforcement memorial for Illinois fallen officers. As we arrived at the memorial, they added Illinois State Police Trooper Brooke Jones-Story to the wall. Zechariah had run for Trooper Jones-Story earlier that year.

Following the Memorial, Trooper Jones-Story's husband noticed Zechariah, approached him, and they embraced. Following that moment, he gave Zechariah the hat he was wearing with a Wonder Woman W on it, which honored his wife. It was a powerful moment for Zechariah and the mission. It was the first time we experienced what traveling as Running 4

Heroes meant to surviving families outside of our home state.

After we left the memorial, we resumed our commute to the hotel. At the request of our friends from Peacekeepers, they wanted Zechariah to arrive carrying a flag and finishing a mile for all of Illinois' fallen heroes. We arrived at the starting point of the run, which was exactly one mile from the hotel entrance. Upon arriving at the run location, dozens of law enforcement officers were waiting for Zechariah's arrival. Zechariah got out of the car and shook the hands of every first responder who was there to greet him.

After taking a few moments to express his gratitude, Zechariah grabbed his pole and flag to position himself for the run.

The weather was clear when we arrived in Illinois, though the forecast called for rain throughout our stay. As Zechariah was preparing for his mile run, clouds started to roll in, and the wind began to pick up. While it never rained during the run itself, midway through the run, the intensity of the wind caused the flag to rip away from the flag pole. Despite being midrun, Zechariah understood the importance of recovering that flag and getting it off the ground. Zechariah and a fellow officer stopped in their tracks, turned around, and retrieved the flag. They carried the flag for that final half mile, arriving at the hotel together with the flag held high.

When we awoke the next morning, it was very overcast. We weren't sure if the weather would permit the ride, but they decided it would happen—rain or shine. There was only a drizzle when we arrived at the starting location, but the forecast said it was supposed to pick up. When the opening ceremony for the ride began, we noticed the mist had gone away. By God's grace, there was no rain for the four-hour ride.

After the ride, we mingled with everybody, and they presented Zechariah with an award. The award Zechariah received was an appreciation for all of his support and efforts. They wanted to give him a unique award and presented a bust of Abraham Lincoln – who was from Springfield. Zechariah still has that Lincoln bust on his shelf in his room. The mayor also gave him a proclamation and a giant, wooden blue-line flag. That was the first acknowledgment he ever received.

A bagpiper from the Chicago Emerald Society Pipes and Drums Band attended the event. That gentleman, Jason Stubler, played the pipes and would become one of our first-ever board members for Running 4 Heroes.

Originally, we were supposed to fly Allegiant Airlines to return home after the ride. Earlier that morning, the gentleman who coordinated everything pulled me aside and asked if we had flexibility in our schedule. I told him we didn't because I had to be back for work that Monday, and the 4 pm flight with Allegiant was the last flight back. We had no other options. The guy informed me they had a considerable sponsor for this event. He said this gentleman lived in Daytona Beach – an hour from where I live. He had his own business and jet, flying up and returning after the event. He agreed to fly our family back home on his jet so we could attend the closing ceremonies.

At this point, Zechariah wasn't into aviation like he is now, and flying made him slightly nervous, but he thought it could be cool. My wife, Susan, always gets anxious when she flies commercial, and the smaller the plane, the more turbulent it seems. She was pretty nervous about it but said, "This is going to be an opportunity for him, and how often do you get to fly in a private jet?"

I told the guy, "You all paid for our flight home on Allegiant; I'd hate for you

guys to be out that money." And he said, "We are still getting you home - just in a different way."
It was impactful to feel the love and appreciation from a place we had never been to and experience something like this for the first time.

Zechariah still had on his Skechers and his Tunnel to Towers tee shirt. It was just before things started to evolve. It's one thing to be told how much you are appreciated online, in emails, and in letters, but it's different to go to a state you have never been to and to see these agencies giving you a standing ovation and survivor families wanting to meet him. Illinois would continue to play a significant role in many ways for us.

The Relentless Mile

On November 6, 2019, Zechariah did a mile called the *Relentless Mile* to honor seven-year-old Abigail Arias.

Abigail was born June 28, 2012, to parents Rueben and Ilene Arias, and she had a brother, Ethan. She was a very joyful, loving, energetic child. At four years old, she was diagnosed with stage IV Wilms tumor – a type of cancer that attacks children's kidneys. When they found it, the cancer was throughout her body and lungs. The doctors warned the family that it would be hard to fight at that stage and that they would have a long road ahead. They did everything they could to fight her cancer.

She went through a year and a half of treatments, which would include chemo, radiation, and surgeries, and in October 2017, she was able to ring the bell. The word to describe her (and her battle word) was "Relentless."

However, six months after they rid her body of cancer, it returned and would be terminal regardless of treatments. Doctors urged the family to make as many lasting memories as they could. They relied on their faith and tried to give her the best life possible.

Ray Garivey, the local police chief of the Freeport Police Department in Texas, heard about her story and wanted to find a way to comfort them, so he invited them to their department's annual "Pancakes with Santa." The event also included a first responder's toy parade.

Abigail loved seeing all the smiles and happiness, and she left there wanting to become a police officer. A few months later, on February 7th, 2019, Abigail was sworn in as an honorary officer and given badge number 758. The way she would write the five was inverted. A video of her swearing-in was shared on social media and went viral. Millions of people saw the video, which is how Zechariah learned about Abigail.

When he heard about her battle with cancer, he continued to follow her story and prayed for her. He had a mental connection with Abigail because she was the same age as Zechariah's sister. Sometimes, he would talk about how difficult it would be if it were in Chloë that situation.

After being sworn in, Abigail traveled across the country, meeting with other officers and agencies – being sworn in by other agencies. She visited with the

NYPD and touched many people's lives, including Zechariah.

Fast forward to November 5th; sadly, Abigail lost her battle with cancer, but, as her family says, she went to be with her Lord and Savior. As much as they prayed for a miracle, the family held fast to their faith. Their prayer was answered through the gift that their daughter has touched many lives and continues to touch lives. Even though her physical body was no longer here, her spirit still existed through so many people.

When Zechariah heard she had passed away, he got emotional and cried. He said, "Dad, I want to run for her, can I?"

So I contacted some local officers and agencies and asked if they would join us if we did this run for this girl who died from childhood cancer. Across the board, they all said, "Absolutely." After the run, when Zechariah was talking on video, he broke down. In the history of doing these runs, it marked the first time on camera during a live run that he could not contain his emotions. After the run, we treated that flag the way we treat every flag – we folded it and sent it to the family, and we have remained closely connected with them ever since.

On November 6, 2019, Zechariah ran the Relentless Mile—the mile for Officer Abigail Arias, mile #293 of the mission. Hers was the last mile Zechariah would run that was not specifically for a fallen firefighter or police officer killed in the line of duty.

When Zechariah spoke at the end of the video, not a dry eye was left. I was behind the camera crying, and my wife and the officers were crying, too.

https://www.facebook.com/Running4Heroes/videos/1486926618112036

You don't always know how a child thinks. On his own, he said on the run video, "Abigail was seven years old, and I did seven laps – every lap honored every year of her life." I never even thought about that, yet as he was running, that was what he was thinking about, "This is her first year …this is her second year …this is her third year…."

After this run, we talked to him about how emotional it was. He was very confident that he was strong enough to do the runs, but in that moment, many things made it feel so close to home to him. We have continuously monitored that, especially on the emotional runs. At the same time, my wife and I have felt that the harsh reality is that there will be those moments when you lose somebody you love, or something happens to somebody you care about.

While it is hard to see, as long as you have the proper support system, it's healthy for the human body to go through those times. If my wife got emotional at her mom's funeral, does that mean she wouldn't go to the funeral for her dad because it is too hard for her? No, you still go, but we made a point to show him extra love that night, and we didn't jump right into another run. We gave him time to process and decompress.

We had many people reach out and check if his mental state was good, and we responded that *just because someone shows emotions doesn't mean they aren't mentally strong*. Even police officers have gone to crime scenes where it has caused them to weep. Even Jesus wept.

Abigail's impact was so influential on Zechariah and this mission that her spirit seemed to find its way into the mission even years after this run was concluded – her story would continue.

Following her run, we decided to stick to our guidelines since we knew we were growing. The mission naturally grew.

At first, Zechariah did these runs, and as the mission started to get known, people wanted to sponsor flags. However, people now saw him as a great representation of our first responders.

Chapter 12

T2T to R4H

As the mission grew, I realized we needed a team to help oversee the mission. I got with some local folks who were supporters of Zechariah's mission. One was the wife of a captain who served in a neighboring agency. She talked about the importance of doing more for injured first responders and about how her husband was involved in an incident where he was struck while stopping traffic at the scene of an accident site.

Someone was not paying attention and nearly killed her husband. After returning to full duty, he still had issues due to those injuries, which made their life difficult when he could not work.

She wanted to start something to help injured first responders but didn't have the platform to make it happen. With everything she shared with me, I thought this could be a powerful part of this mission. Yes, we were honoring the fallen with the flag mission, and I asked myself, "What if *that* is where we used the extra funds?"

We continued to expand upon this idea, and after adding a few other folks to the team, we had our first board meeting on July 1st, 2019, and incorporated Running 4 Heroes Inc. as a 501(c)(3) organization.

One of the first things we looked at was "Running 4 Heroes". When I created the Running 4 Heroes page, I just picked a cool name and *ran with it* – no pun intended.

Would the name be available to create our organization? I researched and found no other organization by that name, so we officially registered our organization as Running 4 Heroes.

I also researched what goes *into* starting a nonprofit and learned quickly that it wasn't cheap to establish one. None of us on the board had served on a non-profit board before, so we were headed into uncharted territory. We had never written bylaws or articles of a corporation or filed for tax-exempt status, so there were many unknowns, but we knew we needed to make it happen.

Our secretary then, Victoria Stonebreaker, was passionate about this mission. Victoria and her mother owned a real estate company. They decided to sponsor us for the fees associated with becoming a 501(c)(3) so that the first few thousand dollars we raised would be used for what it was intended to do: assist in getting the flags we carry to the surviving families. We hired an attorney to help get our non-profit formed. It took about three or four weeks to get our confirmation, but we were allowed to backdate when we were *established* from our first official board meeting in July.

Our goal was to start helping injured first responders while still funding the flag mission. We also saw the importance of Zechariah meeting with the families, which went hand in hand with our mission. I didn't want to wait until funds were raised to issue a grant and then wait longer until we had enough for another grant—my goal was that once we started the grants, we would be consistent.

For the rest of 2019, we fully established our 501(c)(3), and around September, Zechariah ran his *last* Tunnel to Towers 5k. That is when we made the hard cut-off from raising money for the Tunnel to Towers organization and began raising funds specifically for Running 4 Heroes Inc.

Zechariah's goal that year had been to raise $15,000 for the Tunnel to Towers Foundation, and we wanted to present that check at the Orlando run in September 2019.

At the Orlando Tunnel to Towers 5k, we presented a check for over $100,000 to their foundation. Zechariah far surpassed his goal of raising $15,000, which ended our collaboration in a powerful way.

At that run, the race coordinator knew Zechariah was setting out to raise funds for *his* organization and that it would involve travel. They called for Zechariah and Chloë to come up and presented them with suitcases. Zechariah's was custom-made with a blue line and his initials ZC. He still uses that bag as a carry-on when he travels.

One of our first big travels as an established non-profit was a trip to Dupage, Illinois. Sherrif Menderick of Dupage County and his wife wanted to support Running 4 Heroes because we had already run for a few of their officers, so they launched a Running 4 Heroes 5k. What made it special was that present at the run were surviving families that Zechariah ran for and didn't get to meet when we were in Springfield.

Meeting with those families was tremendous. One particular gentleman was the father of Deputy Jacob Keltner, who was lost in the Line of Duty on March 7th, 2019. When he began talking to Zechariah, he broke down; when he broke down, so did Zechariah, and then *everybody* started breaking down. The two of them then shared an embrace. You can see Zechariah's emotion during this moment in a photo taken.

Keltner's flag was only the second flag Zechariah had sent after the flag mission began.

DOCHA Photography

Protecting the Mission for Zechariah

When we created the organization, it was my goal to set it up in a way that ensures Zechariah can remain a part of it, even long after I no longer was. Because of Zechariah's age, he was not legally allowed to be the Founder or serve on the Board of Directors. So, we created the organization with myself, listed as the sole member and founder, so our family was never removed from the mission. Still, we ensured that he would become the Founder when Zechariah was of age. We have it written in our bylaws in the following way:

Chad Cartledge will be the sole member of this corporation. When Zechariah Cartledge reaches the legal age of 18, he will become the founder.

We set up our bylaws so that a vote will not be required when Zechariah legally becomes of age. Zechariah is the founder, and that title will be legitimized on paper. He will also have the power to decide how he wants to be in charge of the organization. The day he turns 18, he could say, "Dad, you're fired." He will have that right. However, Zechariah has said that he has no interest in being the organization's CEO, but what he wants to do when he is 18 is to be a voting member of the board of directors. He wants to be able to select the grant recipients and be a part of the group that makes all the decisions; he doesn't want to operate it.

My initial goal in leading this mission was to ensure he would have that opportunity, and it remains a big part of why I do the work I do today.

Chapter 13

The First of Many

After forming the board, we began having various fundraising efforts to build up enough support to fund our first Injured First Responder Grant. We wanted the contributions to be significant enough that the family could feel the impact. Our goal was to launch with a $5,000 grant and be in a position to ensure a $5,000 grant every month. We also needed to secure enough funds so that Zechariah could deliver these grants to the recipients, which meant some traveling.

From July to December 2019, many of our fundraising efforts were made through social media. We started *travel challenge* when traveling to events, and we encouraged folks to donate as part of those challenges. Zechariah was on the Cross-Country team, and whenever he had a meet, we would also host a challenge—if he finished in the top twenty-five, we would get commitments of people donating $25 or something along those lines.

We did the same thing with his soccer matches – challenging folks to contribute if his team won. His team was good and expected to win often, and we generated many funds for the mission.

By the end of 2019, we had raised just under $40,000, and in January 2020, the board met to select our very first Injured First Responder Grant recipient.

One of the first Injured First Responder Grant applications we received was for an injured officer out of Illinois. We had done a lot of runs for Illinois up to this point, so it made sense that our first grant went to an officer there. We selected Officer John Cebulski of the Aurora Police Department as our first grant recipient. In 2019, there was a mass shooting at the Pratt Warehouse in Aurora. Officer Cebulski and another officer ran into the danger and were overcome with gunfire. Thankfully, no officers were killed, but Cebulski was struck and severely injured. Sadly, many innocent folks were lost in the shooting before officers were able to stop the threat.

The board decided that Officer Cebulski's bravery—running towards the gunfire and nearly losing his life—was such a powerful story and that he would make a significant first grant. I don't think he even knew of our organization. Someone else had submitted an application for him to be considered, and when I called him to let him know he was chosen as a recipient of the first grant, he was moved to tears.

Zechariah and I booked our flights and headed to Illinois. It had just snowed, and Zechariah had never seen snow before or been to a place where we had to wear a sweater. We stayed with Jason, who was on our Board of Directors at the time, in Naperville, and I will never forget this: his backyard overlooked this major golf course, and when he opened his back door, everything was white!

Zechariah went out there and made snow angels and threw snowballs. He was enjoying life! The following day, we went to the police department, and Zechariah presented the grant. Present for the grant were various news outlets, Officer Cebulski, and the Chief of the Aurora Police Department. Zechariah spoke to a large group about this officer and delivered our first *Injured First Responder Grant*. Afterward, we treated Officer Cebulski to a meal with his family before returning. Officer John Cebulski was able to return to duty sometime after the incident, but unfortunately, his injuries forced him to retire early.

One of my favorite videos from that short trip is when one of the officers, after the presentation, was outside in their patrol car. He got out, and he and Zechariah started having a crazy snowball fight! Zecharaiah got him good when a snowball hit the officer right where his shirt and pants met. The snow went down into his pants, and he screamed, "Oh, that's so cold!"

He ran and got in his patrol car, and Zechariah kept throwing snowballs at him as he drove off. We shared that video on social media, and people could see that while Zechariah was traveling and processing adult things, he was still a kid enjoying himself.

Knowing that traveling would be a part of the mission, we decided as a family that school must remain Zechariah's priority. I was also employed on Mondays and Fridays, 9-5, and I needed to be aware of my paid time off. The best way to do that was to develop a travel schedule, and the plan was to fly out Friday evenings and either fly home that Saturday night or early Sunday. Zechariah wasn't missing school for all of these grants being given, and I was not missing work. Zechariah had such high energy that he was never worn out – he loved it. It can be exhausting, but the adrenaline got me through the first year. Seeing the impact this mission was making on others was quite moving, giving me an even greater purpose for seeing this mission succeed.

Increasing the Grants

In February, the second grant recipient that we selected was a firefighter in Lubbock, Texas. He was struck by a vehicle on the interstate. The vehicle also struck another fellow firefighter and a police officer, and both died in the incident. Zechariah had run for both of them before we gave the grant to this firefighter, Matt Dawson of the Lubbock Fire Department.

Zechariah got to present the grant to the wife of Firefighter Dawson, and we met the surviving family of one of the fallen heroes he ran for who was killed in the incident. It marked the first time our mission went to Texas, and it was powerful for Zechariah to meet a surviving family of someone he had run for because even though he had met a few families, it wasn't often, and we were beginning to travel more.

Sadly, Firefighter Dawson would pass away in 2023 as a result of the injuries he sustained. Zechariah went on to run a mile in his honor shortly after his passing.

Between January 2020 and December 2023, we kept our promise to give at least one grant each month—some months, we provided two. By March 2019, we were giving an additional $1,000 to our Grant Recipients when we presented awards.

Not only did we keep the promise of giving grants of *at least* $5,000 each month, but in July of 2020, we bumped it up to $7,500, and starting in January 2021, we bumped it up once again to $10,000 per month, making it an even bigger impact on the lives of injured first responders.

How the Grants are Chosen

During the first six months of 2020, we created an application form on the website for people to submit an injured first responder grant request. In the beginning, *every* application was reviewed during the board meetings, but as more came in, it was necessary to have a grant committee review all the applications first. Once reviewed by the committee, *they* would narrow down the applicants that would be presented to the board for review. After a discussion, board members would individually vote for the recipient they felt needed the grant the most that month. After all the votes were tallied, the application with the most votes was the one the board would select as that month's injured First Responder Grant recipient. We would continue to use this method to select grant recipients moving forward.

God Intervention

In April 2020, the board selected Deputy Gary Coble of the Knox County Sherriff's office in Tennessee as our grant recipient for the month. Before his injury, Deputy Coble was in pursuit of a subject, and the driver tried to run him off the road. Deputy Coble's patrol car struck a power pole, and the crash was so hard that the engine slammed into the seat.

God reminded us that He orchestrates the *timing* of the grants when given, and Deputy Coble's grant was proof of this. I called Deputy Coble and told him he was selected as our April grant recipient, and he started crying over the phone. That's expected because of what this means to them, but he said, "You won't believe the timing of this… since the injury, things have been hard for us. It will be a while before I can even consider returning to duty. And just a couple of days ago, I was sitting in my recliner and felt a drip of water land on my head. I looked up and noticed our roof leaked. All I was thinking was, 'God, we can't afford a lot right now and can't afford to have the roof replaced,' but I knew we needed to act soon."

Gary had called a local roofing company to inspect the roof, and just an hour before my call, the quote from the roofer came in and was just over $5,000. I was calling to tell him about the $5,000 grant just moments after he received the bad news about the roof. We could have selected him for any other month, but just when he called out to God, God gave him *Running 4 Heroes*. I am proud that Officer Gary Coble is back on full duty and has fully recovered.

Another one of our earlier grant recipients was Officer Samantha Hodgson of the Bryant Police Department in Arkansas, who was injured due to gunfire. Officer Hodgson received our Injured First Responder Grant in June 2020. My co-author, Jen Billington, interviewed Officer Hodgson, who shares her testimony in this book and talks about what the grant meant to her and her family. I won't go into too much detail about the incident, but I'll share that the uniform shirt she wore the evening she was injured is now hanging up in our Tribute Hall. She is back to full duty as the school resource officer at her daughter's high school.

Our Injured First Responder Grant continued through early 2024 and has totaled nearly $500,000, with grants being awarded to injured First Responders across the nation, including as far away as Alaska!

Chapter 14

A World Pandemic

In 2020, the world was rocked by the COVID-19 virus, which changed many things and made a major impact on the future of our mission.

When COVID occurred, the Officer Down and US Fire Administration pages were initially slow to add names. Once they started adding the names for COVID-19 deaths, Zechariah wanted to ensure that each hero added still got their mile run.

In 2019, Zechariah ran 376 miles, but he ran for two years of fallen first responders, so we were confident he wouldn't get close to that mile count again. We figured that number would be cut in half. We were expecting 150-175 miles for 2020. Between January and February, Zechariah had logged 37 miles before we got hit with the pandemic. The COVID deaths began hitting the Officer Down Memorial page at the end of March.

Zechariah's first run for a COVID-19 death was on April 4th for an officer from the Chicago Police Department, Officer Marco DiFranco. He ended up doing 17 miles for COVID-19 deaths in April. In May, it picked up even more and continued to grow.

Not only was Zechariah's mile count picking up, but it also impacted other aspects of our mission. There was consideration on whether or not he would continue running because the public's fear of the pandemic brought all the unknowns. Everyone was supposed to stay inside, although the CDC said that getting outside for some exercise was still recommended but that everyone should keep a safe distance.

The pandemic changed life for everybody. What really brought the seriousness of COVID-19 to reality for Zechariah was when schools closed down, and he was forced to attend school at home. He no longer had that interaction with fellow students, which was a change of pace. My wife and I were forced to relocate our offices from Full Sail University and begin working from home. We had to transform our entire living room into an office, and to this day, our living room still serves as my wife's office since her job remained an at-home job following the COVID-19 pandemic. Zechariah's bedroom was converted into a school classroom.

The change of pace was challenging, but one thing we learned very quickly with both our kids (more so Zechariah) is that because he is a high-functioning child with ADHD, socialization is a *good* thing for him. He operates better in a classroom at school. He didn't do as well at home. It became a lot easier for him to get distracted on his computer and not be able to focus as he could in a classroom.

So, it was harder for him as far as school goes, but the school board relaxed many of its requirements because it knew many kids would struggle at home with such a change, and it was a lot more forgiving.

The Downside

Everybody was experiencing something brand new, and it was quickly taking over the nation. COVID-19 deaths were climbing quickly, and vaccines were now highly recommended, though not necessarily required.

Regarding the runs, if an officer was present, we had to change their involvement once COVID-19 became a reality. If an officer came out, they had to stay in their patrol cars, windows up – they couldn't interact with us. That was a bit of an emotional hardship for Zechariah because he loved having the officers run with him and was now being told that he had to run by himself. He got through it, knowing they could still be present, though it weighed heavily on him having to limit his interactions with our local heroes.

His sister, Chloë, was the only one allowed to run or walk with him. That's where he got his emotional support, so if you notice, every time Zechariah runs and passes his little sister, he gives her a high-five.

Another thing that made it difficult for us was the elementary school where we held the runs became one of the locations where they would conduct vaccine drives. The hours of the drives would frequently overlap with the times in which runs were scheduled, so we needed to plan the runs around the times in which the school bus loop was not being occupied.

Where we got a lot of backlash was how COVID-19 impacted our Injured First Responder Grants and the decision we made for travel. Some states closed off the ability to travel, and some said only travel if required. As a family, we always believed in living our life to the fullest. If you are feeling perfectly well with no signs of illness, to be locked up in your house is government overreach.

We live in a free nation, and to not be able to go outside because it might be too dangerous – well, my family has the freedom to make the decision on if we feel it's too risky or not to travel. We felt that as long as Zechariah and I were healthy and not showing any signs of illness and as long as we adhered to the requirements, we would continue to travel. So we talked to the Board of Directors, and we all decided that as long as the place we were going to allowed travel, we would continue to do the grants.

Masks on a Plane

Only a couple of grants had to be mailed, and we had to postpone the actual presentation – both were in California.

When we traveled, we followed all the requirements, but there was only one thing I did *not* like about traveling during that time frame - wearing a mask on an airplane was not enjoyable.

The airflow isn't that great, and you are confined in these tight little seats. It was frustrating, and I am so glad that requirement disappeared. I was glad we could pull down our face masks if we ate or drank. We would take our time with those bags of peanuts.

I was one of those who spent ten minutes slowly taking a sip …and another sip…

…slowly.

They give you a little bag of peanuts, and you usually eat three or four at a time because they are small, but during the mask requirements… one …at …a …time.

And I didn't just eat the peanut; I let the salt melt and let the peanut sit in my mouth. I treated that peanut like a mint. And if they came by, saying, "Mask, please," I'd say, "Oh, I'm eating," and place another peanut in my mouth.

One of the reasons we didn't worry about flying is that nobody *else* was flying. People were so afraid of flying that we would have flights almost entirely to ourselves. There were times that I would have a section of five rows, and Zechariah moved to the second section of five rows on the other side of the plane because there were possibly seven or eight people on the flight. Also, during that time, all the airlines were required to step up their sanitizing process, so it was safer being on a plane than stepping into a gas station.

By God's grace, Zecharaiah and I *never* experienced any medical issues. We never once had Covid symptoms. Now, there was a short period when my wife was diagnosed with COVID-19. She tested positive when we were on a trip and returning from a grant we did in South Carolina. Susan called to tell me she tested positive when Zechariah and I were heading to our connecting flight home.

My first thought was that we were around her a few days before, so I let the people in South Carolina know, but fortunately, no one there got sick, and Zechariah and I never showed any symptoms. Susan picked us up, and we tried to stay to ourselves. The first thing we had her do when we arrived home was to take us to get tested. Both Zechariah and I tested negative.

To Vax or Not to Vax

The next thing about the pandemic that became a topic was getting vaccinated. Many organizations pushed that, and I will tell you, I am *not* pro-vaccination. That is another thing I think should not be forced upon us – especially a rushed vaccine, and we did not have enough time to see the impact of the vaccinations. I'll be honest – we were very anti-vax for a while.

During the entire year of 2020, we had never been vaccinated. We didn't feel pressured to get vaccinated, but unfortunately, there were some travel changes where certain *places* required vaccines if we were to travel there. It was a decision we did not take lightly. Canada was a place that was talking about bringing Zechariah up there for their memorial because we had started adding Canada's officers and honoring their fallen in 2021. We would be required to have the vaccine to travel outside the country. We also had a cruise that we had planned prior to the

COVID-19 pandemic, and they also required proof of vaccination.

We talked about it as a family, prayed, and decided to get the vaccination.

These were some of the negative things the pandemic brought, but as far as the running aspect of it, I mentioned Zechariah had run 376 miles in 2019, and for all of 2020, he still ran a mile for all of the COVID-19 deaths of first responders. He ended up running 401 miles in 2020. He ran more miles in 2020 than in 2019, when he ran a combination of 2018 and 2019's fallen officers and firefighters.

As we neared the end of November 2020, my wife and I decided this was too much. We addressed the Board of Directors and told them we needed to change how we did the COVID-19 runs. At this time, Zechariah was the only kid running. We needed to find a solution to bring down the mile count while still giving those heroes the honor and respect they deserve.

We came up with the *COVID-19 salute*. Beginning in January 2021, we kept a log of that prior month's losses classified as COVID-19 deaths. The COVID-19 Salute would be a non-stop three-mile run – 21 laps around the track loop. Zechariah carried the blue and red combo flag as it would honor *all* First Responders. For every death added from COVID-19, my wife and I would fold a flag for all of them.

One month, there were 92, so we folded red flags for firefighters, blue for law enforcement, green for border patrol, and gray for correctional officers. We would place the flags in a clear bin and show them on camera before a run, and Zechariah and an officer would escort that bin to a lead patrol car that would patrol behind him for those 21 laps. Even though Zechariah didn't run with each flag on the run – all of the flags still went on that run with Zechariah.

Each flag was part of the salute and still honored the families' hero, and with the flag was a note that Zechariah signed. For the individual miles, Zechariah (and now the other kids) hand-wrote notes to the fallen First Responder's family, but we knew there would be 60-80 a month for the additional miles for COVID deaths, so we printed a note that he signed. There was still that personal touch. Looking at the log spreadsheet, in 2021 alone, Zechariah would have run 850 miles total had he run all of the miles as individual miles with the COVID-19 additions. He still did 325 miles in 2021, even with the COVID-19 salute being done in this way.

Throughout 2021, he kept consistent, running that three-mile run every month starting in February. We continued that throughout 2022 until about May or June 2022, when we noticed a change in the line-of-duty COVID deaths in March or April of that year. It seemed things were under control, and healthy people were no longer *dying* from COVID. We rarely see a COVID-19 Line of Duty death now. So, we decided around May that we would not do monthly COVID salutes and would plan to honor future COVID deaths at the end of the year.

For 2023, we talked about the process of COVID-19 deaths moving forward. A few of us thought about having the runs be individual miles again, but after establishing a COVID process, it wouldn't be fair to those 600-700 heroes who didn't get an individual mile. When we change the policy, unless it makes sense to change it back, we should continue doing what we have been doing. So, beginning in 2023, the plan was to do a COVID-19 salute annually (and we would have a wall at the Tribute Hall dedicated to those heroes so their families could still see their heroes' names on the wall).

Necessary Changes

COVID changed the way we did things. It changed the way we did the runs that first year, the way we acknowledged line-of-duty deaths from COVID-19, the way we traveled (and prevented us from traveling to certain places), and the nature of what we did because COVID was always in the back of our minds.

And especially for me, going onto the Officer Down Memorial Page every day in 2020 was discouraging –when we thought we were caught up on the miles, they would add several more deaths of First Responders the next day. There were many evenings when Zechariah was running three individual miles. We honored every First Responder who was considered a line-of-duty death on the national level.

This shows the commitment Zechariah had. Even during his summer months when kids were out of school, Zechariah would run mile after mile. A lot goes into planning and conducting these miles. In September 2020, Zechariah ran 52 miles. He hadn't even turned 11 yet and was as busy as if on a *concert tour*.

He was so committed and passionate about what he was doing.

While Zechariah was conducting runs and traveling, many kids lost the opportunity to socialize during the pandemic. Because of the mission, Zechariah did *not* lose that opportunity to socialize. When kids returned to in-person school, some had to learn to communicate with others again because they spent the entire year and a half only communicating with their families. But because Zechariah could still travel and officers could still come out, he could have that interaction and an advantage other kids didn't have. He didn't lose social skills because he was still socializing, which worked well in his favor.

More Positives

COVID was a big reason we are the mission we are today – and *that* is a positive. It forced many people to work from home, which was true for my wife and me.

In 2021, I spent the entire year working in the front room of our house. I was a supervisor and things ran smoothly as long as my team did the job right and I stayed on top of my responsibilities.

While at home, our team transitioned to remote syle of training. My team was very self-sufficient, and I could rely on them to do their jobs. This lessened my stress, and I could focus more on Running 4 Heroes in between doing my job. We doubled our donation size that year.

Much of my vacation time at my job was used toward mission work and never really used for vacation time for myself. By 2021, we began discussing that if we continued Running 4 Heroes, we would eventually need somebody to operate the ship full-time. I give the period during COVID a lot of credit for helping make the transition to leave my job to work full-time running the organization.

If I had not been able to work from home, the Tribute Hall/Headquarters would not have happened. Those who were pro-law enforcement hated the shutdown rules, and when everyone was scared to leave their house, seeing this kid choosing to do this mission despite COVID-19 still encouraged others.

Despite all the hardships brought on by COVID-19, Zechariah was still going out there and honoring First Responders while people were disabled with fear. People saw that this kid was legit. Unfortunately, many heroes' lives were lost due to Covid, but there *were* some positives.

Another reason those runs were crucial during the shutdown, and one of the reassurances we received that we made the right decision to continue the runs, was that no funerals were being held.

One of the most significant impacts COVID-19 made was that while people were not gathering, memorial services were not happening. When first responders were killed in the line of duty, people could not honor that hero properly for their service.

On at least three or more occasions, families contacted us after watching the run video of their loved one and would say, "Thank you, your video was the *only* service being conducted that I had to honor my hero."

Communities came together to watch these runs, which was their only memorial service. We filled an essential void for surviving families.

What we didn't anticipate at this same time was the potential danger for Zechariah after George Floyd's death.

Chapter 15

A World Gone Mad

Disclaimer: I will not use this as an opportunity to discuss my viewpoints on the George Floyd incident. I believe mistakes were made, and I will leave it at that. However, the purpose of the George Floyd discussion is strictly to discuss how it impacted the way we conduct our organization.

The George Floyd incident was negative for law enforcement across the country. Riots and protests were happening throughout the United States, and there was a big turn against our law enforcement officers. Some of those groups that turned against law enforcement took it a step further and would even protest against the events of *supporters* of law enforcement.

Our mission has always been about honoring our first responders— including our law enforcement officers, and once the riots began, they expanded beyond Minneapolis.

As a board, we had to sit down and talk about the safety of our runners. As things started to get crazy violent, even our local communities talked about protests - some in our county, some in Orlando, which made national news, and a few board members felt we needed to postpone the runs to let this blow over temporarily. I had reservations about that because COVID was adding many more miles. Had we taken even a month off, it would have been impossible for Zechariah to get caught up.

We can't postpone line-of-duty deaths. We would still have officers losing their lives, and if we could not honor them, the list would be too extensive. A couple of things that we had to take a hard look at were, first, the physical location of where we conducted the mission. There were protests across the state and even peaceful, well-put-together protests in our county.

There was no clear evidence indicating that where Zechariah would run would be in jeopardy of being a hot spot for protests. We live in one of the safest cities in the state of Florida, and that is something we take much pride in.

Despite the George Floyd incident, our community stood behind our law enforcement. They knew our officers had been adequately trained to handle those situations. So we had to think about Zechariah running in a place that wouldn't cause him danger.

The group felt that where he was running was very safe. We didn't think that there was a threat. However, we also know that even the safest communities are not immune to protests. We still felt we needed to safeguard Zechariah if somebody saw a run announcement posted and decided to use that run as the place to make their statement.

We created a new game plan for the mission's new norm. One of the most significant changes we made was the involvement of having law enforcement present at the runs. Early on, when the mission first started, local First Responders *wanted* to be involved. Before we incorporated this change, there were times when we would have a dozen officers at some of the runs if they could come out.

However, after a year into the mission, there were times when nobody was available to assist. Zechariah had done the runs without sirens, lights, or officers present before. After the George Floyd incident, we felt that could no longer be an option. We felt that if we were going to do the runs—especially since we announced them publicly before they happened—we would need an officer there in case we had protesters for Zechariah's safety.

Taking Precaution

At least one law enforcement officer will be present for Zechariah (and every child who runs). Today, we always include that the run will only happen if we have law enforcement present. We have even held the start of runs in the past while we waited for a local officer to become available and assist us in honoring our fallen.

The second change was our travels and bringing Zechariah into some communities where protests were big and made national news. We did a grant presentation for an officer in Ramsey County outside Minneapolis. I guess you could say it was the *luck of the draw* that the month that we selected that officer to be our grant recipient was the same month they had the Chauvin trial.

The day of the presentation was the day the Chauvin trial might go to the verdict stage, and there were many protesters – it was unbelievable. The board decided that we could not publically announce where this grant is. We could only say we had an announcement to make, but it would come after we had already done the presentation and Zechariah was there.

We had a former board member who was an officer permitted to carry on an airplane join us for this particular trip. Zechariah always had somebody armed around him for his protection during this particular mission trip. It was almost like Zechariah had a bodyguard.

Zechariah wanted to conduct a run in Minnesota, so we worked very carefully with the Ramsey County Sheriff's office to complete the run securely at one of their training facilities.

Susan wasn't very concerned with the local runs because we lived in an area where we had never felt in danger, but *this* was different now. When she learned the board voted for us to go to Minneapolis during the Chauvin trial, she was the most prominent advocate for *not* announcing the runs. Susan wasn't a big fan of us going, but knowing we would always have somebody armed, she was calm but wanted us to check in frequently. That one had her a little bit nervous.

During the flight to Minneapolis, she requested we not wear our *Running 4 Heroes* shirts or anything that indicated we were with the mission. We knew he could be a target if someone knew who Zechariah was. I promised her we would only wear something that indicated we were with Running 4 Heroes once we got to the venue.

From arrival to departure, the Ramsey County Sheriff's Office did a great job ensuring we felt safe. We didn't stay overnight this trip—we flew in and back out that day. Our goal was to honor our fallen while awarding Deputy Dallas Edeburn, one of their heroes, with our Injured First Responder Grant.

Sadly, Deputy Dallas Edebur tragically died of a heart attack in the line of duty in 2022. Zechariah would go on to run a mile for him just over a year after presenting him with a grant.

What stands out more to us about the trip to Minneapolis is that this hero was someone we got to spend time with. We learned that he and his wife were expecting their first child, and Deputy Edeburn discussed his desire to return to duty. We took time to learn about who he was as a hero, which we brought home– not fear or uncertainty. We brought home the feeling that we could do good for a hero who needed it, though sadly, this hero would succumb to a heart attack related to the injury that made him eligible for the grant.

Can't We All Get Along?

As a mission, we see the most backlash from those against law enforcement. We get people coming to our socia*l* media pages frequently, saying that cops are bad and the blue line flag is racist - some even asked if we would do runs for individuals who were killed by the police. The answer is no. Our mission is to honor first responders lost in the line of duty.

If someone doesn't understand what our law enforcement is faced with, try going through a simulation where you are the officer and have to make split-second decisions and see if you, as an officer, go home that day. I'm not saying that *all* law enforcement officers are perfect, but they have a hard and thankless job, and the majority are here to protect and serve.

Mean People

Some folks who learned of Running 4 Heroes were not always kind. Many of them took to social media to verbally attack my son. Zechariah's face has been featured in memes on anti-law-enforcement groups, which has led to dozens of people coming onto our page with anti-police rhetoric.

Zechariah has probably been called a boot-licker over a hundred times. We don't expose him to all *we* see. Even so, he has *not* had to deal with a lack of support from his community. Even in school, his teachers have always supported him. There are good relationships between our police and our schools. There is mutual trust and respect for one another. We feel blessed to live in an area where Zechariah has always felt that support.

Another thing that erupted during this time frame was the notion that police are racist. The truth is if you flip through the binders at the tribute hall and take the time to look at the faces of the first responders we have honored, you will see *every race* and every walk of life.

We are *not* racist; we keep true to our mission statement - we honor *every* first responder killed in the line of duty. It doesn't matter their color, belief system, or gender identity - all that matters is whether they are first responders and whether they lose their lives serving their communities.

Zechariah has also dealt with an occasional heckler. I think one was in Texas, hollering as he ran by about not understanding why the road was closed for a run. The heckler had some choice words, but Zechariah ignored them. I guess because he knows the truth, he doesn't let the negative side of the world stop him from doing what he believes in.

I feel God has had His hand on this mission. Despite a pandemic and an anti-police movement, Running 4 Heroes was still able to thrive and be a blessing to so many hurting families.

Chapter 16

Girl's Best Friend – The K-9 Mission

Running 4 Heroes was growing, and our first expansion, Running 4 Heroes K-9s, occurred in 2021.

Lieutenant Erik Lloyd with the Las Vegas Metro Police Department was one of the officers Zechariah ran for in 2020. His end-of-watch date was July 29, 2020.

In late 2020, we received a message from Lt. Lloyd's wife. The run Zechariah conducted to honor her husband moved her;

they planned another run for his honor in Las Vegas and wanted Zechariah to join the event. At this point, Zechariah had never been to Nevada for the mission. We flew out and met the Lloyd family, and Zechariah participated in the run.

One family that came to the run was a young girl named Theresa Ann and her parents. We had already heard of Theresa because she had her own little project called "Love with Lemons," in which she held lemonade-stand fundraisers for officers. Theresa began when she was about three years old, and over six or seven years, she had raised several thousands of dollars for First Responders and K-9s. She had a significant place in her heart for the K-9s.

Theresa attended many events in Nevada, and several officers knew her. She knew the Lloyd family, and she wanted to meet Zechariah. It was asked if Theresa could run with him, and we said, "Absolutely." We thought it would be fun to see another kid running with Zechariah.

Zechariah and Theresa Ann 2021

Working Together

We loved meeting Theresa and learning about her efforts. We stayed in contact with her family. Her dad, Robert, had let us know that Theresa couldn't do the lemonade stands anymore because of COVID restrictions, but she still wanted to do something to support law enforcement.

Theresa noticed that Zechariah only ran for *people*, not dogs, and she wanted to run to honor the K9 heroes killed in the line of duty. Robert asked me what it took to start a non-profit, and we discussed options for Theresa. I told him that we wanted to expand our outreach and honor K9s, but with all the COVID-19 deaths, Zechariah could not take on more miles as the only runner.

Robert wanted to continue funding K9s with equipment and vests. Still, since *Love with Lemons* was never an official 501c3 and with the high costs of starting a non-profit, I suggested that Theresa do the runs under the Running 4 Heroes banner and incorporate them into our team.

We talked about Theresa running for the K9s; we would create her logo, and they would be part of an already established organization. This would allow them to raise money for the K9s immediately and eliminate the wait and the costs. It was a unique opportunity for us both. We had never had anyone else conduct the runs; it's always just been Zechariah.

Theresa would run a mile for every K9 killed in the line of duty. She joined us midway through 2021, and we lost about seven K9s that year. Her first task was to backtrack and honor every K9 we had lost.

Getting Started

There was a K9 lost in 2016 that Theresa felt very close to, and her request was for her first official mile to be for that K9. That K9 was K9 Nicky of the Las Vegas Metropolitan Police Headquarters. K9 Nicky was lost on March 31st, 2016, after being shot and killed while attempting to apprehend a subject. Her passing shook Theresa's core, and K9 Nicky has remained in her heart ever since.

Since that first mile was logged, Running 4 Heroes K9s has sadly logged over 90 miles for K9s lost in the Line of Duty. We have also given over $35,000 in K9 equipment to K9 officers nationwide.

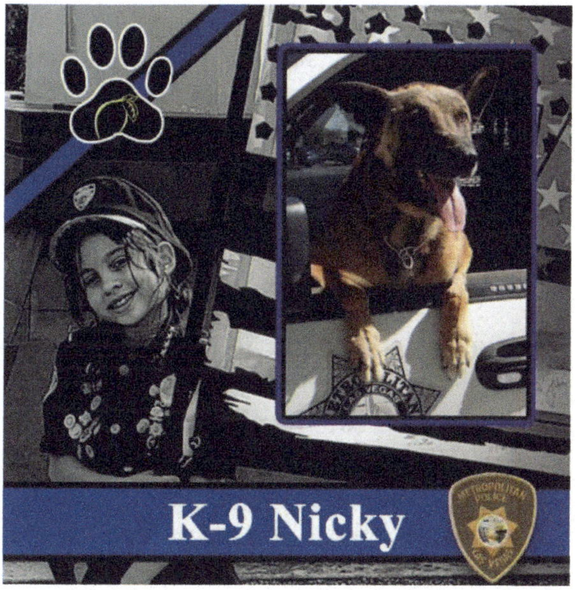

First official run for 2018 fallen K9, Nicky.

We know the reason we came out to Las Vegas is because God continues to have His hand on this mission. There just happened to be an event, and it just happened that the Lloyd family wanted Zechariah to come out, and it just happened that that was the same community where Theresa lived.

Not every run we do leads to us going to a state because the family wants us to be a part of something. Still, this run allowed us to get to know Theresa, establish that relationship, and expand our organization.

One of the things we require of our runners is that they can run a mile, and she was able to show that at the run. Our runners also have to have a heart for our heroes, and we could tell right away that Theresa and her entire family truly have a passion for honoring and supporting our first responders.

Blessed be the Ties that Bind

Theresa's story brings us to a remarkable connection.

One of the reasons Theresa wanted to meet with Zechariah is because of Officer Abigail Arias, the young girl who was lost due to childhood cancer. We discussed her story and its impact on Zechariah in a previous chapter.

Theresa first learned about Zechariah when he ran for her friend, Abigail. She met Abigail at an event in Vegas and saw her again at an event in Texas later that year. They became good friends before Abigail passed away. Theresa saw that Zechariah ran to honor Abigail and wanted to meet him when she found out he was coming to her area.

Becoming International

In 2021, we expanded the mission and became International by adding Canada. A couple of line-of-duty deaths in Canada were brought to our attention, and Zechariah was inclined to honor them.

At that point, we didn't want to add any more for him because he was already doing hundreds of miles with the added COVID deaths, but in 2021, after changing the way we did the COVID runs with the monthly salutes, his mile count was cut back drastically.

When the idea of including Canada came to us, we first researched how many Line of Duty deaths they had in a calendar year. On average, they lose two or three a year— not a lot compared to the United States, which is 150-160 yearly.

Having had people reaching out asking if Canadian officers would be considered, and blue-line Canada flags were available to order, the Board decided to add Canadian officers killed in the line of duty.

The first constable we ran for was Cst. Shelby Patton – EOW June 12, 2021. A stolen vehicle struck and killed him while conducting a traffic stop. Following a truck reported stolen from Manitoba, he initiated the traffic stop in Wolseley, Saskatchewan. During the stop, while outside his patrol vehicle, Cst. Patten was struck by the suspect vehicle, and the suspects fled the scene. Cts. Patton had over six years of service and left behind a wife.

Zechariah conducted a run on June 22nd, 2021, at mile #937. Even though Canada typically doesn't lose many officers, sadly, a week and a half later, Toronto Police Services lost Cst Geoffrey Northrop (also struck by a vehicle).

Since the first run for Canadian officers, our Youth Runners have conducted nearly a dozen miles for Canadian officers as of this writing. The addition of miles for

Canada also makes us an International Organization.

Zechariah's first mile for a Canadian Officer 2021

Chapter 17

DC and Police Week

In 2020, the pandemic had brought everything to a screeching halt. Surviving families wanted to meet Zechariah but couldn't because of the restrictions. So, in the spring of 2021, the planning for Police Week rolled around again, but Covid was still being considered around planning public events.

Instead of canceling the annual May event again, they postponed it to October to give Covid a few months to run its course but made it clear that things would be more restricted. We knew that we had to be a part of it no matter what.

Susan and Chloë don't typically go on trips for the mission, but this was one of the few events where the whole family went. We felt it was important for everyone to see the scope of this mission.

We were invited to attend Police Week as a guest of the Middle and East Tennessee Concerns of Police Survivors Chapter. Zechariah had run several miles up to that point for their region of Tennessee, and they wanted Zechariah to stay at their hotel and be with that group. To this day, we tend to stay at the hotel where their chapter stays.

When we arrived in DC, they gave Zechariah the same welcome every surviving family attending Police Weeks would get. When we exited the plane, honor guards lined the gate stretch and saluted as Zechariah walked by.

While walking through the airport, we could not go five steps without one of the surviving families recognizing Zechariah and coming up, giving him a hug, a challenge coin, or taking a photo. It took us an hour to get from the gate to the bus that would take us to the hotel.

When arriving at the bus, we were welcomed with a neat surprise – we had our logo and Zechairah's photo on the side of the TN COPS bus! We had always been a big supporter of that particular COPS organization. We had financially contributed to them from Running 4 Heroes several months prior. Part of our donation to them would help with transportation and getting the surviving families to the hotels and events. We didn't know that they had put decals on all their sponsors' buses, and they had a huge decal of Zechariah's logo that said, "This bus is sponsored by Running 4 Heroes Inc."

Zechariah thought that was cool, and we all felt it reminded us of how important this mission had become to so many.

THIS BUS SPONSORED BY
RUNNING 4 HEROES, INC.

Feeling the Emotion

Before we got to our hotel, they stopped at the host hotel to drop off the surviving families; everyone needed to register. While we were there, that was the first time Zechariah had an opportunity to be around that many survivors who were seeing him for the first time. It was pretty overwhelming. Not necessarily in a negative way, but the goal was to be there for about 30 minutes and get everyone registered, and we ended up being there for a couple of hours.

We couldn't go anywhere without people recognizing him, stopping him, and wanting to take their photo with him. It meant a lot to him because he could see how many people this mission had touched. But it was quite emotional as well—when many people come up to you crying, you are compelled to have compassion. It can weigh on you after a while.

We had to purposely find ways to get away from it all so he could have his time alone. One of the things we did to get away from it was to visit Arlington. His great-grandfather was a WWII and Korean War veteran. He was a Silver and Bronze Star recipient and was eligible for inclusion in

Arlington Cemetary. My grandfather passed away in 2021, and *that* is where he wanted to be buried, so our family ensured he was buried there.

We knew this would be one of the things we could do as a family to break up Police Week for Zechariah and have a few personal moments to unwind. While at my grandfather's grave, he gave him one of his challenge coins. He put the challenge coin down on the side where you couldn't see it. Every time we go to Police Week in DC, we visit my grandfather's grave. Zechariah continuously checks for the coin and will replace it with a new one if it is removed.

Zechariah places a challenge coin at his great-grandfather's grave.

A moment for the family

That week, we experienced the candlelight vigil for the first time, and it was a powerful moment for him. For these vigils, they call out the names of every fallen First Responder that has been added that year, and since they had canceled the previous year, they were calling out names from the prior two years. There were many names, but it was impactful for Zechariah because as he was standing there, he knew and remembered most of the names being called. Seeing all the families, he was able to get a feel for what all of this meant to everyone.

The next day, they took us to the National Law Enforcement Officer Museum. Zechariah was looking forward to it because it was one of those things that would let him get away a bit. It was gorgeous. We went into the room with photos of all the fallen Officers and Firefighters from the previous year, and Zechariah recognized many of them from his runs.

After five minutes of being there, it started happening again—people began recognizing him. He was getting pulled aside; people wanted to meet and take a picture with him. It got overwhelming because he tried to take in the museum, but bless his heart, he also wanted to ensure all the survivors could meet and talk to him. He understood why this mattered.

So, he would take time to meet with the families and capture a photo with them. At one moment, there grew such a large crowd around Zechariah that one of the museum workers came over to see if everything was okay. It turned out that that guy knew of Zechariah, and he even wanted to get a picture. It was a neat experience, but it continually grew increasingly overwhelming for Zechariah.

It's not that he didn't want to meet with these families; it was just a lot at one time for a ten-year-old. Every two seconds to have people going, "Hey, that's the kid…" "Are you Zechariah?..." everywhere he would go, he got that. At first, it was fun, but after a while, it started wearing on him, especially when he needed some downtime. At one point, it became so overwhelming it caused him to cry, and we knew right away that we needed to give him space.

My wife and I realized he had become so well-known that he had lost some freedom. He lost the ability to be somewhere without people recognizing him. But even through the emotions, he handled it like a champ because he *wanted* to meet those families. He knew how important it was to them.

Every year at Police Week, they do two things: a candlelight vigil at night closer to the Washington Monument, then the annual memorial service from the steps of the US Capitol. At the Memorial on the Capital lawn, we intentionally stayed in the back because only immediate families were to be in the front, where all the names were being called. The president was the keynote speaker, so obviously, there was a lot of clearance for anybody too close, so we stayed back and only had to go through metal detectors. Throughout the ceremony, officers walked by, recognized Zechariah, and wanted photos.

Deputy Constable Caleb Rule – this was a fallen hero whose family was close to our hearts and whose name was to be called out at this memorial. Zechariah wanted to make sure he heard his name being called, though we knew his name would be called later in the ceremony. The way they handled the role call of the names for this memorial service is to go by state. Caleb lived in Texas, so heroes from this state had their names called later on in the service.

By the time they reached the names for the state of Texas, many families from prior states had already cleared the area, and the president had already left after giving the opening address, so security was a little more lax at that point. Zechariah was able to get close to where the widow of Deputy Caleb Rule would walk by. He was patiently waiting. Out of the traffic where officers walked to and from, the only people passing by us would be the surviving families after receiving the medal. They were emotional – many tears and the honor guards escorted them to the bus or where they needed to go.

We were waiting for them to call Deputy Caleb Rule's name, and even in the emotional state these families were in, half of them noticed Zechariah and would stop, and they would want to hug him and get a photo with him. But he was so focused on not missing Deputy Rule's name that when they got to about five names before calling his name, Zechariah was still getting pulled aside; he broke down and cried once again because he was afraid he would miss hearing the deputy's name. And that meant a great deal to him to hear his name.

So we talked to one of the officers nearby and asked them to position themselves between Zechariah and them so that if any more families approached, they could let them know that Zechariah would be happy to get a photo with them if they could wait about ten minutes. Zechariah needed that moment.

After he heard them call Deputy Rule's name, Rule's wife Eden went up and received the medal; when she passed by Zecharaiah, he embraced her.

A photo of this embrace was captured right in the moment. We now use this photo for various purposes within the organization. You could tell that hug meant a lot to her and Zechariah at that moment. Out of all the Police Weeks, this photo stands out because, more than anything, Zechariah wanted to give her that hug at that moment.

Having that moment wiped out all the anxiety from the week.

Widow of Deputy Caleb Rule

While the vigil and the Memorial Service were the main reasons we attended Police Week, we also went through the memorial in DC. While there, he looked up the names of Officer Walwyn Stuart, Caleb Rule, Natalie Corona, and a handful of others he wanted to look up. One of the names he wanted to look for was the name James Cartledge, which was the name of my dad and his grandfather (no relation we know of). There was an officer named James Cartledge who was killed in the line of duty in the 90s, and he wanted to find his name on the wall as well.

Overall, he experienced DC in such a powerful way, but in those four or five days, he was made aware of the scope of what he was doing.

We would shelter him from Facebook and the comments, so for him, it is difficult to fully grasp just how much of an impact his mission is making because he doesn't see it every day as we do. We learned that he gets anxious when he is around super large crowds. Whenever he is around large groups, he always finds a place to get away from everybody, and while that is good for his mental health, it looks like he does not want to be there. He *does* want to be there, but there are moments when he gets so overwhelmed with all the people that he will find a place where he can be secluded. Jesus did that, too.

We didn't recognize this about him until the first Police Week because it was the first time he was around such a large crowd of surviving families.

One of the fun things we did to break up the emotional week was to visit the Air and Space Museum. The recognition wasn't as bad there, but somebody stopped him to take photos at least twice while we were there. That wasn't too bad because we could enjoy ourselves and not have people coming up who recognized him every two seconds. If we can do something outside the scope of mission work, we try to – obviously at our own expense, to give the kids some experiences and see a sight the state might be famous for. We might only have an hour to spend instead of a whole day, but it helps to break his mind from the tragedies surrounding this mission.

With this mission, Zechariah steps into an adult role so much that it's good to see him be a kid. Away from the presentations and meeting families, Zechariah is just like every other kid.

Chapter 18

Volunteer to CEO

Using all my paid time off and vacation time from my job to push this mission became quite challenging as the mission continued to grow. There didn't seem to be enough days to accomplish everything needed. I was very fortunate to have a boss who would allow me to leave early to catch flights and not have to use paid time off, and I could make up those hours during the week.

Our family pitched in. My dad would pick up the kids from school, bring them to my job, and drop them off so we could get to the airport, and I would bring our packed suitcases to work. I had a sound support system. They knew this mission was necessary and did their best to accommodate my busy schedule. But there were many events that we couldn't do because I didn't have any more paid time off.

All of my paid time off from my job was used for the mission, rarely for family vacations or personal time. R4H continued to grow, that process became more complex, and the mission demanded more of my time.

The pandemic was a blessing because we were forced to set up our offices at home, and I could dedicate more time to the mission. As a manager, as long as my team was doing their job and I was doing everything that needed to be done promptly, it helped to be at home so that I could do more interviews and take more phone calls for the mission.

If I got an urgent phone call while working full-time, I couldn't take it. I couldn't conduct the Running 4 Heroes business at work. Working from home made that more manageable, but it was as though I were working two full-time jobs, and something had to give.

One of the most significant changes was when the board decided that Running 4 Heroes needed to become my only job. The sheer statistics proved how rapidly we were growing. In 2019, we had been a non-profit for only six months, raising about $30,000. In 2020, we raised approximately $250,000. In 2021, we raised almost half a million dollars. The signs were pointing to another year of rapid growth.

The board sat down with me during the fall of 2021, and we discussed making this my full-time job and did I understand the *risks* of making it my full-time job. There are many risks to having this role. My livelihood for my family would depend on donations to this mission, and if people don't donate, I am out of a job. The board wanted to make sure I fully understood the risks. My job at Full Sail was secure, and operating Running 4 Heroes alone wouldn't give me a safety net.

We didn't want to be a non-profit paying six digits for a CEO. We weren't there yet, and I don't think a non-profit CEO should be bringing home six-digit salaries. I used to feel that non-profit CEOs shouldn't take home *any* compensation, but I have changed my position after seeing all the work that goes into keeping it running and having no time for another job – running a non-profit *is* a full-time job. There's this notion that if it is a non-profit, nobody should be getting paid, and everyone should be a volunteer. I can understand that concept if a smaller non-profit brings in a little throughout the year. Still, when you are a nationally known non-profit generating hundreds of thousands of dollars a year and making an impact across the nation, supporting not just a community but an entire country of First Responders, it is a job. Since starting this mission, I have worked about 70 hours a week.

Even so, I don't think a CEO should make six digits, so we talked about what I felt would be a fair salary, and I proposed that to the board, and they had their discussions. I was not a part of those discussions. It took about two or three months to talk it through, and my fate was unknown then. My employer knew it was being discussed, but we didn't know for sure until the board finally said they came to a vote.

December of 2021 is when we voted on the budgets, and they decided to offer me the position of a paid CEO. Some caveats are that it wouldn't come with any benefits – no 401k, health or dental insurance, or PTO. My salary would be a hard-set salary, not commission-based. If we ever had a year where we raised five million dollars, my salary would remain the same. My salary was under 40-50% of what a CEO of my caliber would typically make. I was okay with that because this mission was never about making money for me, but now, I would be able to grow and expand the mission and take us to that next level.

On January 1, 2022, I began my role as a paid CEO of Running 4 Heroes and left my job at Full Sail University. However, I also lost my voting powers as part of the board for Running 4 Heroes. I still attend board meetings, but as a CEO, I explain the day-to-day operations to the board. This took much stress off because I no longer needed to juggle PTO from another job. If there are conferences to attend or events that Running 4 Heroes should be a part of, I could now attend them.

When I started as full-time CEO for Running 4 Heroes, my office was still located at our house, and it became inundated with *Running 4 Heroes* between 2019-2022. The kitchen drawers were full of Running 4 Heroes stickers, mailers, and envelopes, and our whole front room was our office. My desk was at the front of the house, and we had converted the guest room into our interview room. We put patches up on the walls where we conducted our Zoom meetings. One of the challenging aspects of operating everything from our home is that we have dogs—and loud birds. Basically, we have a zoo, and trying to conduct the interviews or meetings was frustrating.

However, once Running 4 Heroes became a 501c3, our residence became public information. Knowing how easy it was to find out where Zechariah Cartledge lived felt unsafe. I feared that if he ran for an officer in a very anti-police community and somebody didn't care for him and decided they wanted to terrorize him or send him hate mail, our address would be public record. Finding a permanent office for Running 4 Heroes was necessary for safety alone.

I wanted Running 4 Heroes to be located in Winter Springs because it is safe, and I wouldn't lose sleep at night wondering if our building would be vandalized. However, I didn't want it connected to a strip mall. As we grew, I envisioned having a Tribute Hall where we could continue that "honor" beyond the mile run. And if our Tribute Hall were connected to a strip mall, where people might be parking to go into a Subway or a grocery store, it would take away from the personal experience. I wanted something that would give the families their privacy.

A set of nearby business offices had been vacant for over a year. My wife Susan approached me with the idea of checking into that location. We scheduled a meeting with the property manager and took a tour. I could not describe the feeling when we walked into the building—my mind already envisioned things.

We talked to the property manager about the facility and had many back-and-forth conversations regarding terms and logistics. After much discussion with the Board and the Property Manager, the Board felt it was worth the risks, and we agreed to move forward with a 5-year lease.

Once we had the keys, business started – deciding how we wanted the Running 4 Heroes Tribute Hall to look. I was the only one there every day, all day, and one thing I appreciate about the board is that they allowed me the creative freedom to do what I wanted essentially for the tribute hall. I wanted it to be a place to honor heroes and give a glimpse of the history of the mission, which is why a 9/11 section was so important to me. That was the foundation of what started Running 4 Heroes, and it fits very well into the concept of a tribute hall because it would be paying tribute to those heroes from 9/11, which inspired this boy to run these miles to pay tribute to *every* First Responder.

When completed, the Tribute Hall was truly beautiful. I immediately knew just how important this place would be for surviving families. If I had still been working at Full Sail, I don't think we would have had this opportunity, and Susan and I wouldn't have gotten our house back. Ironically, Susan works out of the home, and our front room is still an office. We went from one extreme to another.

Chapter 19

The Tribute Hall Era

Doing More for Surviving Families

During the first board meeting in January 2022, I voiced a need to give more to surviving families who lost it all, especially those who left behind children. I wanted to see if we could give more financial support to the families of the fallen first responders. We had an injured First Responder Grant and provided safety equipment for K9s, but for surviving families—they got a run and a flag—it was in my heart to do more. Don't get me wrong;

the flag means a lot to families, but I wanted to find a way to do something beyond just the flag.

So I approached the board and said, "We have hundreds of thousands of followers on social media, which gives opportunities to reach people through different fundraisers. What if we created fundraisers specifically for the families of fallen heroes, especially when children are left behind?"

The board loved the idea. These fundraisers would be designated solely for these families so that 100% of what is raised goes to them. So, we launched what is called our Beneficiary Fund. When a first responder is killed, leaving a family behind, as long as we have permission from the agency or immediate surviving family, we would start a two-week-long campaign to raise funds for their family.

As a non-profit, we technically don't have to get that permission because it aligns with the mission. But I told the board that I thought we needed that permission because if we created a fundraiser and the agency or family was unaware that we were doing this, an agency or department might post a disclaimer about any other fund-raising being fraudulent.

The agencies need to be aware of and back our fundraiser to prevent confusion or credibility issues with the scammers who run fraudulent fund-raisers. I didn't want to begin a fundraiser for these families without permission.

We started our first fundraiser for the Beneficiary Fund in January of 2022. To this point, we have conducted over 50 fundraisers for families of fallen first responders and have given over $300,000 to these families.

In the first few months of being full-time, we started an effort that has helped many families. We also launched the Tribute Hall, synonymous with Running 4 Heroes. When you think of Running 4 Heroes now, you think of the grants given to surviving families and the Tribute Hall, where those families can come and see their hero honored.

The Tribute Hall

One of my first tasks as CEO was overseeing the building of our Tribute Hall. I knew that when this project was completed, it would hold meaning for so many surviving families nationwide.

The fact that we are not far from Orlando, the tourist capital of the world, assured me that families would visit our Tribute Hall. Surviving families bring their kids to Disney to get their minds off of their tragedy. I know that because I get phone calls from the families asking, "Hey, aren't you guys in the same area? We want to meet you because what you did meant so much to us." We weren't just opening up a tribute hall in the middle of nowhere; we were in a position that we knew would bring survivors to the Hall because they were already coming to the area.

It took about six months for the tribute hall to be where it needed to be. However, we opened our doors immediately on the Headquarters side in March of 2022 for our local police department. The headquarters is offered as a safe spot for our Winter Springs Police Department. They had 24/7 access there, and we provided snacks, drinks, water, a clean facility, and an office room to charge their flashlights and radios and fill out reports. We also wanted this facility to be a place to give back locally.

It was also important to me to have an open-door policy for surviving families. If we had a surviving family in town and they wanted to see what would become the Tribute Hall, I would invite them in, even when it wasn't complete. I wanted them to see the vision. There was a period after they built the framework that we had to cease building while waiting on permits for the electrical.

Our contractor couldn't do anything until we had the permits. It took 30-45 days, which was unbearable because I wanted to continue seeing progress. During that waiting period, it was special that we had a few surviving families come to visit. We gave them a 'Sharpie' and let them sign the beams before the drywall was placed where the memorial wall would be.

When people would visit, they didn't know that even within the walls, survivors left their mark, honoring their hero. That is a silent unknown people don't know about, and it's just a powerful thing.

Building the Tribute Hall included closing off windows, installing a new lighting system, and getting signage approval. Much effort went into this endeavor, and we wanted to make sure what we displayed would be mounted beautifully, bringing honor and respect. We wanted the Tribute Hall to be about the heroes and their families, not the kids. While the kids are the heartbeat of Running 4 Heroes, we are about a lot more, and the Tribute Hall shows that.

The vision for the Tribute Hall was to have a place that allowed us to keep our promise to surviving families – *never to forget.*

Hurricane Ian

We were initially slated to hold our opening on October 1st. Unfortunately, Sheriff Lemma of our local county sheriff department was unavailable, but we got our local police chief. A few folks planned to fly down, and a board member also planned to fly down. It was going to be an extraordinary day for us.

About a week before our grand opening, we noticed a hurricane forming on the south end of the coast of the Caribbean, just north of South America, possibly heading our way. Hurricane Ian would wreak havoc on our plans. It went under Cuba, heading north, and then cut, leading right through Florida just south of the I-4 Corridor, where we are located.

Ian hit a Category 5 status; its highest winds were 160 mph, so there were many questions about how it would impact us. There were signs that it sped up and might come through a little earlier than expected, which it did. It made landfall in Florida on September 28th. We weren't sure if we should cancel because we had been through enough hurricanes that blew in, and nothing was damaged, and we didn't want to cancel without reason.

We decided that with the storm's severity, even if that Saturday were beautiful, parts of our neighborhood would likely get some damage, and all of our first responders would be tied up. It wouldn't have been fair to them, especially knowing many would have to work through the night for several nights. We felt it would be best to postpone our grand opening, which meant plans had to change for some folks.

Some who would make it on the 1st couldn't make it now because of the date we would reschedule. Looking back, we made the right call because, despite the beautiful day, our community had significant flooding.

Fortunately, our home wasn't flooded, but we did have minor flooding in the Tribute Hall, and we found an issue with the roof that Ian unveiled. It took about two hours to clean out the water from the Tribute Hall. We had much work to get ourselves back where we needed to be to open and decided to have the grand opening on October 15th instead.

As it worked out, our sheriff was available that day and was now able to be our keynote speaker. And it tied in well with our Gala because the Blue Tie Gala was that following Saturday, the 22nd. So, we were able to have a kick-off to Gala week with the grand opening of our Tribute Hall and were able to promote the Gala. We had another soft start on the 21st for those here for the Gala but couldn't attend the grand opening. It was also Zechariah's birthday.

We opened the doors on Oct. 15th; the ceremony was beautiful, our Sheriff provided a keynote address, and we had the singing of the National Anthem. Seeing the emotion of the people who walked through, looking at the names on the wall, reading the stories and learning about these heroes, and touching the steel and artifacts from the WTC site meant a lot to them.

In that first couple of weeks, we had some key people in our lives show up. The families of Officer Natalie Corona and Officer Abigail Arias walked through and saw how we were honoring their daughters; there were such raw emotions, and it reassured us that we made the right decision to invest the time and resources into the

Tribute Hall. The board allowed me to design it and bring forth the vision I am passionate about. I wanted to find a way to make this an honorable, respectful gesture for these grieving families. That was important to me.

Chapter 20

Youth Runners

One of the most significant changes we made In 2020 (and the scariest) was the introduction of adding other kids to run for fallen first responders. Though we already had Theresa running for K9s, this would be different.

Zechariah was beginning to get burned out. He was now in Middle School and thinking about High School, wanting to participate and be involved. He went to dances and played a killer saxophone with the band—he just couldn't do it all. His heart didn't change for the mission; he still wanted to be a part of our mission, but his heart was in many places.

After several years of running 1,100-1,200 miles, it starts to wear on you—especially since we aren't just talking about the running but the *emotions* that go into every mile, knowing another life was lost.

It was getting to the point that being open to running every night was exhausting. When we traveled for the mission, it would take a few days, and then Zechariah returned, having to catch up on the miles he needed to run. Sometimes, he'd have to conduct back-to-back three *individual miles* in one evening. It was a lot, and Susan and I promised we would not push him to do this. Zechariah knew he could let us know if it was too much.

The board and I discussed getting Running 4 Heroes to a point where it did not solely rely on Zechariah. How many followers followed the page specifically for Zechariah or the mission itself? If we introduced other children, would they embrace them like Zechariah? It was a risk, but it was necessary.

Locals - Jayden and Giuliana

Fortunately, a few local kids came out to run with Zechariah, so they knew the routine. We had a kid named Jayden and one named Guiliana. They would consistently run with Zechariah. Guliana had logged over 100 miles running with Zechariah, and we decided to experiment and let these kids do the official miles. In May of 2022, we gave them a trial run to see how it would go. Because they were local, I was still behind the camera recording and speaking anytime they did a run, so the transition was pretty easy.

They were nervous for their first runs, but the response was overwhelming as our supporters welcomed these kids as they did Zechariah. They were glad to see the other kids stepping up in something Zechariah had started. One of the things that comforted me was that after Guiliana did her first run, she got a letter from the Chief of the firefighter she ran for, and he told her how much that run meant to them and provided her with a patch. Giuliana has also had the opportunity to meet with surviving families whose hero she has honored, a moment that I know meant everything to these families.

Adding the local kids went well, but how would we handle kids running *outsid*e of our community?

Texas – Anthony

Anthony had met and ran with Zechariah during our trips to Texas. He wanted to do one of the official miles for a Texas officer. We had to figure out how he could do practice runs where his parents could upload a video and send the link or upload it onto the page – a lot goes into it. I was a nervous wreck the first time there was an out-of-state run I wasn't there for. It was a bit emotional, too, because up to that point, I was a part of every single mile ever conducted. It required *letting go* on my end and trusting the process that we created.

When Anthony did his first mile, his turnout with the local support was *phenomenal*. Every time he runs, he gets such a great turnout from the officers. We gave his family access to the page to upload their videos directly. When I got the alert that the video was posted, I immediately watched it. There were many emotions – first, the sense of pride. We had kids in other states furthering the mission of Running 4 Heroes. There was also a sense of comfort, knowing I didn't have to do it – it was taken care of. For three and a half years, every one of our evenings, we gave up doing the runs.

There I was, sitting in my house, watching the video and realizing we had gotten to that point where other kids and families could do this. That was powerful. And to see Anthony personally delivering that flag and how the family responded, knowing it wasn't Zechariah, meant a lot to me.

I will always be proud of Zechariah for having the heart to start this mission and see it through to the point of handing off the baton, though he is still involved. I am just as proud of our youth runners, who are not my children. It has never been about notoriety for Zechariah or these kids—the mission was about finding a way to use these kids' passions to do good in the world by honoring our fallen.

Anthony and Jayden are no longer runners for the mission, but I remain forever grateful for their efforts to honor our fallen. I know their impact on the surviving families whose heroes they honored will last a lifetime. Anthony and Jayden will always be heroes in my book.

Georgia – Andrew

Seeing Anthony's run sparked a desire for Andrew to conduct a run. Andrew did not have the connections with local agencies as the other runners, and we worked through some of the logistics with his grandparents. They were concerned about how it would work out, so they went to their local agencies and told them they hoped to become a part of the mission. The agencies immediately knew about Running 4 Heroes and were excited to learn that one of their incredible community youth members would join the cause. This gave Andrew's grandparents a sense of confidence, knowing they were joining something that already had such a positive exposure in their community.

Andrew trained and did his first trial run, and we knew immediately that he had the heart to honor our fallen. It didn't take him long to begin running officially for the mission.

He usually does his runs around his neighborhood, and since joining the mission officially in late 2022, Andrew is already approaching 100 miles conducted to honor our fallen. God bless his neighbors, especially when they have the firetruck out;

they are loud. It's fantastic that his neighbors come out and watch him go by, and we are so grateful that they support him. We are also thankful to the Hall County Sheriff's Office, the Gainesville Fire Department, the Hall County Fire Department, and the Georgia Highway Patrol for supporting Andrew.

New Jersey - Morgan

Bernadene, one of our board members, introduced us to Morgan. Morgan has also always had a heart for canines, which is very similar to Theresa, but Morgan is closer in age to Zechariah. We were introduced to Morgan when we were scheduled to be in Delaware, and Zechariah ran a mile in New Jersey with Morgan in September 2022.

Man, she was a runner. She kept up with Zechariah the whole time – in fact, you could tell she was holding back. We could tell she had Zechariah's same passion, desire, and determination. That evening, we asked Morgan and her mother if Morgan wanted to become a youth runner. A smile lit up on Morgan's face; you could tell she was excited. It was interesting that Morgan and Zechariah had the same personality.

They like all the same stuff, and they were two peas in a pod that night.

Morgan was excited to be a potential youth runner and is also nearing 100 miles, which are conducted to honor our fallen heroes. We continue to have support from her local agencies, from the Ocean County Sheriff's Office to the Pioneer Hose Company to the Brick Police Department and even the New Jersey State Police.

New York – Matthew

Matthew joined the mission in 2023 after learning about Running 4 Heroes through a friendship with Andrew's grandparents. From the moment Matthew first submitted a video for consideration, you could tell he had a heart for our First Responders.

Residing under the jurisdiction of the NYPD, Matthew is known in his community for the support he shows his local heroes. It was no surprise to learn that he wanted to do his part to ensure that those who have fallen in the line of duty are also honored beautifully.

Matthew has been such a blessing for this mission, and we are honored to know that he will be helping us pay tribute to our heroes in the years to come.

Hawaii – Raiden

Raiden came to Running 4 Heroes after following the mission for quite some time. However, Raiden was no stranger to the First Responder world. He was known across the state of Hawaii and even on the mainland for supporting First Responders.

Knowing how much of an impact he has made nationwide, we were thrilled to learn that he wanted to continue supporting our heroes as a runner for the mission. When his family reached out, we immediately began the process of training, which didn't take him too long. He was quickly brought on as a Youth Runner, and his efforts were immediately embraced by his friends with the Honolulu Police Department, who joined him as he conducted his miles.

Raiden's impact has been felt throughout the nation since first conducting that first mile. We are blessed to have Raiden as part of the Running 4 Heroes ohana.

Illinois – Zachary

Zachary is our newest mission runner, residing in the state where we first presented an Injured First Responder Grant in 2020.

His parents reached out, sharing their son's desire to be part of the mission. Zachary came from a First Responder family and had a passion for running. After a few short discussions and after getting the blessing of his hometown agency, the Braidwood Police Department, Zachary began submitting run videos for consideration—and from his very first mile, we knew he had the heart and stamina it takes to honor our fallen.

He quickly joined the ranks of the Running 4 Heroes mission and has already made personal impacts on surviving families, including personally delivering flags to the widow of a fallen hero he recently honored. Seeing those moments once again reassured me that the mission is in great hands, with kids like Zachary leading the charge to honor our fallen.

Having these other kids step up was a risk. We would learn if people were supporting the mission or Zechariah. It became evident that they supported the mission. They love and support Zechariah, too, but they are just as excited to see other kids following in his footsteps. Let me share the following message I received recently.

"Hello. My husband was shot and killed on March 12, 2023. We received the flag and generous donation from Running 4 Heroes. Our son Karson is ten years old and has been inspired by this, and he would like to know how he can join Running 4 Heroes and participate in running for other fallen heroes! If this is possible for him to do, please contact us!"

I'll contact the wife of this fallen hero and will share with her the steps we require for youth runners to be selected. Still, I can't help but get a little emotional at the thought of a surviving child running in honor of another fallen hero as part of Running 4 Heroes. The mission I lead is doing God's work. I genuinely believe it.

In a world where kids spend most of their time in their bedrooms playing video games, these kids are getting active and doing something to make a difference. At the time of this writing, we have eight official youth runners: Zechariah, Theresa, Guiliana, Andrew, Morgan, Matthew, Raiden, and Zachary.

Knowing now that supporters have embraced our youth runners assures us that this mission will reach beyond Zechariah and his youth. Zechariah will always have a place in R4H – his childhood silhouette will always be our logo, but the fact that other kids are doing this means so much.

Giving Back to Our Youth

We are doing our part to ensure these kids know they are appreciated, and we launched the "Zechariah Cartledge Scholarship Fund." Zechariah isn't eligible for it, but for these kids, for every 25 official miles they run, they receive a $500 scholarship from Running 4 Heroes. A couple private donors are matching those scholarships as well, and these scholarships can go toward any schooling they choose.

We want to support their life dreams because they are giving part of their childhood to support these heroes. I hope people realize that when they support Running 4 Heroes, they are also helping support the future of these kids. Our youth runners are giving up their time to support these heroes, and we want to give back to them and support their goals. I initially clarified to the board that Zechariah isn't eligible for this. Many people felt he should be qualified because it was his mission, and he had put much time into it. When they presented the idea of naming it the "Zechariah Cartledge Scholarship Fund," I agreed. If any scholarship was named after our founder – that's the place to put it.

2022 was a big year for us. There were many question marks and uncertainties, but it became evident that the Tribute Hall and adding these additional youth runners helped solidify this mission's future.

A Change of Plans

Unfortunately, a declining economy led to a change in our support for 2023. While the number of supporters grew, folks could not contribute as they once had. And I don't blame them; even a combo at a local fast-food chain costs nearly $10.

We also began to have issues in our facility. For various reasons, we needed to leave early. This change was a hard one for us, especially me, as so much time, effort, and energy was put into building a Tribute Hall that, for two full years, provided comfort and healing to surviving families.

In February of 2024, we closed the doors to our original Tribute Hall and moved into a new location. We plan to reopen the Tribute Hall at a new location.

We promise our fallen will not be forgotten. While it may take a while to get to the point where we can once again open our doors, we haven't stopped doing what this mission does best– honoring our fallen. Through the challenges we faced in 2023 and into 2024, we have continued to ensure every fallen hero is honored with a one-mile run, and we have grown our Youth Runner count.

Our promise has never changed, and our purpose and vision remain the same. We know that we are in a time of testing, which God allows us to experience to remind ourselves to trust Him through it all.

Chapter 21

Experience - the Best Teacher

Some experiences stand out more than others, and a few of those must be included in this book.

In November 2019, Zechariah was invited to NYC to be on the GMA3 with Strahan, Sarah, and Keke. They brought him on their special called "Thanks for Giving," where they get folks from across the country to show how they give back, and Zechariah was one of the ones they would feature. It allowed Zechariah the opportunity to talk about his mission. After spending time asking about why Zechariah started the mission, they had a surprise that we didn't know about – they had several surviving families in the audience.

They started talking about some of the heroes that Zechariah ran for, and they said, "We have two of the wives of those officers here," so they stood up in the audience and came and joined us on the stage. They embraced, and Zechariah got to talk with them a bit, and I know that meant a lot to him. As part of that week, GMA3 wanted to do something nice for their guest, and they surprised Zechariah by thanking him. They found out that Zechariah is a big Arizona Cardinals fan. They said, "We have a special message for you," and they showed the monitor. Kyler Murray was on it and said, "We love what you do, we think it's great, and we want to show you our appreciation by bringing you out to Arizona so you can attend one of our football games. As it turns out, the game they gave him the tickets for was when they played the Steelers – my favorite team. I'm thinking, "Whoa – what did I do to deserve this?"

I felt guilty because I was going with Zechariah and should have been pulling for his team. Still, I wasn't—I was pulling for my team, so I felt like a horrible dad. But I told Zechariah that *that* would be the only game if the Steelers had lost and that I would have been okay with it (but the Steelers won). It was a good game, though, and we enjoyed ourselves.

NASCAR

NASCAR has always been something Zechariah enjoyed, and to this day, he is still a big NASCAR fan. One race team, particularly Mike Harmon Racing, was a pro-law enforcement team. They had a car they would race in the Xfinity Series that always supported various aspects of law enforcement. One of the members of the race team contacted me in 2020. They had met Zechariah a year prior and said they would like Running 4 Heroes on their car in Daytona. We were very excited; however, I clarified that I wouldn't use the funds we raised for the mission for sponsorship purposes - this was not something I wanted to use the donations for; we were still trying to build our grants.

They said they wanted us on the car and would make it work. We partnered with several supportive businesses for Running 4 Heroes, including Gresco, Honor & Respect, Support 1, Nella's Cottage, ZagBag Board, and others wanting to fund this car.

However, even with their support, we would still come up short. I brought it up to the race team to have a name badge for every first responder who lost their lives in 2020. They had done that with a car previously with breast cancer survivors and ribbons. It would be awesome if we could make this car a tribute car for every hero lost in the prior year.

Zechariah ran 402 miles for 2020, so we had 402 badges on this car -red for firefighters and blue for police officers. What made it unique is that the names on the car were handwritten by the spouse of an officer whose name was on the car - Officer Jason Knox of the Houston Police Department, who was lost in a helicopter crash. We got the car funded, and it took to the track.

It was an interesting race weekend because it's a lower-funded car, and we had to qualify on time. We didn't have a cushion of points and had to race our way in. By just a few tenths of a second, we made the field. It ran the Daytona, and we watched the race from a restaurant just down the road from the track. Unfortunately, our car was involved in a wreck, but it worked out in our favor because they reuse all of their equipment for all of their races; if the car had remained intact, that sheet metal would have been reused for another race, but because we got involved in "the big one" in which half the field is taken out in a crash, there was enough damage done to the car to where it wasn't salvageable. And because of that, we obtained the hood of that car, which we now have on display at the Tribute Hall.

Come Fly with Me

Another experience that stood out was that Zechariah found something he loved through this mission, and that is the love of traveling, aircraft, and flying. Until recently, that is all Zechariah wanted to do in the future - be a pilot. In 2021, we went to Midland, Texas, to give a grant. A Reserve Deputy for the Midland Police Dept. is a private pilot for a family living in Midland. He was in town the week we were there. He thought taking Zechariah up in the jet would be neat, and he reached out to the family who owned the plane.

Zechariah got to sit in the cockpit seat and control the aircraft for part of the flight. I watched him shift the controls to the left, and you could feel the plane turning to the left. Fast forward to the following year, and we announced two grant recipients in

Texas in the same month. An officer from the San Antonio Police Department and a Firefighter outside Midland were getting grants. Our original plan was to fly into Midland, do the Firefighter grant Saturday morning, drive the 3-4 hour drive to San Antonio to do that grant later in the afternoon, and fly back home from there.

We had yet to book a flight when one of our board members who served in the Midland area contacted me, and they knew the pilot. He said, "Hey, the pilot heard you were coming, and he would be in town that week and wants to talk with you." I called him, and he had talked with the plane owners and worked it out to fly us to San Antonio but told me there were two caveats. Caveat number one – the family who owned the plane wanted a handwritten note from Zechariah telling them about the mission. Caveat number two was that Zechariah would sit in the co-pilot seat again and help fly the plane.

Zechariah was super excited. The Midland officer who received the grant the first time we went to Midland flew to San Antonio with us to witness the other grant. So she was on the plane with us. Once we got to 2-3,000 feet altitude, Zechariah took the rest of the climb and pretty much controlled the whole flight just before landing. He even got to control the rutters while we were on the jetway and got to lead us to where the plane needed to park. After we did the grant presentation in San Antonio, we hopped back on the plane – this time at night, and he got to fly us back to Midland.

We got to experience him flying us both during the day and at night. That experience meant a lot to him because it solidified his passion and what he wanted to do.

Close Call

One of the grants that stood out for us was for Deputy Will Halvorson, who served with the Lynn Co. Sherrif's Office in Iowa. We went to Iowa for an event in 2022. Will was one of the deputies on shift who served as an escort to help us get to the hotel, and we spent some time with him. Zechariah really bonded with Will during our time with him.

Just eleven days after we got home from Iowa, we got messages about an Iowa officer who was down. It was Deputy Will Halvorson. He was responding to a call of a robbery in progress, and as he walked into the convenience store, the guy exited the store and shot Deputy Halvorson at point-blank range, and he fell straight to the ground. He was able to radio one quick call, "Officer down." The guy thought Halvorson was dead, and he felt around for his gun and took off with it. The moment Zechariah found out it was his friend, it crushed him. He asked to talk to our board and told them he wanted to give him a grant. It was important to him.

The board selected Halvorson as a grant recipient. Less than two or three weeks after coming home from Iowa, we were hopping on a plane to return. This grant made an impact on Zechariah because he got to know this officer pretty well. To almost lose him shortly after seeing him gave Zechariah great pause and reinforced even more that what he does is so vital to the families of the first responders.

Other experiences included seeing some neat places: he saw the Golden Gate Bridge in San Francisco, trekked to the top of Pike's Peak in Colorado, and retraced the steps of Steven Siller (Tunnel to Towers) in New York City. However, two of the trips that stood out for us as experiences we will never forget are the trips for the mission to Puerto Rico and Alaska.

Puerto Rico

Puerto Rico was sponsored, and Felicia TSU PR Inc. (Todos Somos Uno Puerto Rico) brought us out. One of the events Zechariah was doing there besides visiting the Police Memorial was to conduct a mile run in Old San Juan. When we arrived, they had live music—a blend of instruments.

Puerto Rico's music hints at Caribbean, African, Spanish, and Taíno influences—from salsa and merengue to plena and reggaeton. We were welcomed like we had never been before. It was pretty incredible.

Sadly, as we were arriving in Puerto Rico, they had an officer who was shot. The original report they put out was that he died. We talked about how if it were true, we would be here for four days - let's do the run here. We found out later that the initial reports were wrong – he did not die but was severely injured. I will never forget the family reaching out to us and requesting that we be part of a prayer vigil they were having outside of the hospital.

After Zechariah did one of the events, they immediately got us to the hospital through a police escort. Zechariah and two of our board members got to take part in the prayer vigil for that officer, and it was pretty special. Aside from just how beautiful Puerto Rico was, the highlight of that trip was that they closed down some city roads that they had never closed down in the history of Old San Juan so that Zechariah could do his mile run.

At the entrance of the port is the Casa Del Moro. They closed down the long dirt path that leads to the entrance, usually covered with pedestrians and tourists. Zechariah would start the run right at the top of that pathway in front of the castle to the police memorial, which was right at one mile. They got the approval from the local government to do that. Zechariah carried the blue line Puerto Rico flag for that run. The setting, the scenery, and the amount of support Zechariah received made that run memorable. We continue to be grateful to the commissioner of the Puerto Rico Police Department for helping us put on a memorable run – one that we will remember for a lifetime.

Alaska

In January 2023, we announced our grant recipient for an officer out of Anchorage, Alaska, which would involve traveling in early February. Alaska in February is COLD. We're from Florida (70-75 degrees in February – quite beautiful). Traveling to Alaska - the overnight low was -11. We have never experienced negative temperatures before. It's hard to buy winter clothes in Orlando – they're non-existent. We had to go to a Brass Pro Shop and purchase gear that is probably more designed to keep the bugs off, but you can use them as winter gear. When Zechariah did the one-mile run, the temp was 2 degrees. There was a snowstorm two days before we got there, but it was sunny on the day of the run. Zechariah was navigating ice patches on the roads. In Florida, we don't have snow shoes.

It was one of the slowest runs he had ever conducted. He ran the whole thing – but it was more like a jog because he was sliding some. When we walked out the door that first morning in Anchorage, I expected it to be a stabbing-pain-cold, but it felt more like a 40-degree day in Florida. It doesn't feel as cold because it's dry and not humid, but when the wind blows – you feel it. It's very easy to trick yourself into thinking it is not cold. I took off my gloves, and in five minutes, I wondered why I couldn't feel my fingers!

Fortunately, we were only briefly there and were in the air as much as in Alaska. In that short 24-hour period, we saw the start of the Iditarod Trail Sled Dog Race. It travels from Anchorage to Nome, entirely within the US state of Alaska, roughly 1,000 miles long. Most of the teams finish in less than ten days. We happened to be in town during the start of that event.

We stayed up late on our only night there because the Northern Lights were supposed to show up, and sure enough, we saw them. It was brief, but we saw the Aurora Borealis.

On the way back to our Airbnb at two in the morning, we almost struck a moose! In less than 24 hours, we had a full Alaskan experience.

A Presidential Nod

Another memorable event at the very start of the mission was when Zechariah was recognized by a senator in Arizona who requested to former President Trump that

Zechariah be considered for the Presidential Medal of Freedom. Even though Zechariah didn't receive the medal, he was honored to receive a letter from President Trump highlighting what Zechariah was doing and that he was being considered for the high honor. To get acknowledgment from your nation's leader was quite extraordinary.

The Reach

So many more experiences stand out in our minds, but it means a lot because it helped define Zechariah's future and also helped show us a perspective of the reach. From meeting the family of Officer Natalie Corona to delivering that first grant to an injured officer in Illinois to being interviewed by Mario Lopez and Michael Strahan – we've had many neat experiences that we will not forget. It just solidifies the importance of what this mission is about and what it means to folks across the entire country and even to the islands in the Caribbean - it just shows the reach and the impact.

I had somebody message me about eight or nine months ago. They were on a cruise to the Cayman Islands. The gentleman wore a Running 4 Heroes shirt, and an officer in the Cayman Islands approached him and said, "I follow that kid in the States."

Another thing that showed Zechariah the scope of his reach was when we took a family cruise in 2022. We visited Cozumel, the Grand Cayman Islands, and the Costa Maya. We got to swim with the dolphins during one of the stops we made in Cozumel. Before the excursion began, we went through an introduction to prepare us, and the group before us was taking off their gear.

A gentleman from another ship in the previous group approached us and said, "You're that kid who runs the miles, aren't you?" Zechariah said, yeah, and the man said, "I'm an officer from Louisiana, and I told my wife I thought it was you, but she said, 'There's no way, we are in Cozumel Mexico.'" They got their picture with Zechariah, and things like that continued, assuring us that this work was essential.

Zechariah has been to over 40 states doing this mission, so he has seen much beauty in the United States. Moreover, he has been able to touch hundreds of thousands of lives across this nation.

The First Annual Memorial

Another powerful moment for the mission was on April 26th, 2022, when Running 4 Heroes conducted its very first memorial service. During the service, we unveiled our Platinum Signs and Designs Memorial Wall, honoring the lives of every first responder we ran a mile for. Sheriff Dennis Lemma had opening remarks, and police chief Matt Tracht provided keynote addresses, as did the mayor, Kevin McCann.

We had bagpipes, the Central Florida First Responder Bagpipes and Drums Band, and an invocation by Seminole County Sheriff's Office Chaplain Walter Person. It was a 30-minute memorial held in the parking lot of Running 4 Heroes with about 100 chairs.

Surviving families came from as far as Houston, Texas—the widow of Sgt. Ramon Gutierez donated a motorcycle helmet and uniform we display in our Tribute Hall. We had the family of Deputy Blaine Lane, a Polk County sheriff's deputy, in attendance, and the family of fallen Apopka Fire Department Firefighter Austin Duran. Also in attendance was the family of the fallen Florida Fish and Wildlife

Conservation Commission Officer Kyle Patterson.

We had the Seminole County Police Department Honor Guard and Winter Springs Police Department Honor Guard present the colors. After the service, the color guard escorted the surviving family members into the Tribute Hall and gave them about 20-30 minutes of private time to see the memorial first. They allowed them to reflect, and they stayed by their side the entire time.

Then, we opened the doors to the public. The families of Gutirez and Duran hadn't seen the display we set up for their loved ones, so in addition to seeing their names on the memorial wall, they got to see the display that had their heroes' uniforms or bunker gear for the first time. It was an experience that will forever be ingrained into my mind.

There were a lot of nerves involved with the preparation. We live in Florida, and knowing the memorial service would be conducted outside, we wondered if the weather would cooperate. Typically, the rains or storms don't hit Florida until later in the afternoons, and we were starting early, so I was pretty confident that the weather wouldn't hinder the event.

Several city commissioners attended, and many local agencies had representation there. The one thing I couldn't secure was someone to sing our National Anthem, and it was suggested that I do it myself, as many folks know I was a singer. I was a little nervous to do it because I didn't want this to be about me, but many people reminded me that if I did the National Anthem right, no one would think it was about me. There are ways you can do the National Anthem that make it about *you*, but if you sing it traditionally, people focus on the anthem.

When all was said and done, the memorial service marked an important moment for the mission, and we will continue to do so once our Tribute Hall reopens in our new facility.

Uniform Delivered

Every time we get a uniform for the Tribute Hall, it's emotional. Still, when I heard the family of Officer Natalie Corona would donate their daughter's uniform, I thought I did a good job preparing myself for the feelings I would have when it arrived. I will never forget when the mail carrier knocked on the door and delivered the package.

When I saw the return label of The Corona Family and that it had Natalie's picture – the same picture that Zechariah saw on the news that inspired him, I started weeping. As the mail carrier left, I heard the key code pressed on the front door and saw an officer approaching the Headquarters side. I couldn't let an officer see me in that state, so I walked into the Tribute Hall and headed to the Firefighter room where nobody could see me. I just sat and cried, knowing the contents inside – it was hard. I composed myself and started to open it, and bam - it started again. I had so many thoughts going through my mind at that moment.

One of the thoughts that struck me was that she only had a few uniforms. Sadly, she was killed wearing one of those uniforms and buried wearing one, so there was a good chance that the one I held might be the last one she came home in. It was yet another powerful reminder that we have made such an impact in the lives of these families that we've honored that they trust us with something so personal so we can continue to tell their heroes' stories. That envelope meant so much to me that I never threw it away.

2023 Police Week in DC

We had attended the memorial in DC many times. In 2022, Zechariah did a mile run in Washington, DC, but what made the 2023 visit to Police Week special was that Zechariah was given a huge honor. He was allowed to present the rose for all fallen heroes, which he would place on the wreath honoring every fallen officer.

They go through every state and call that state's fallen hero. As they call their names, the families come up, are given a beautiful medal, and place a rose on the two wreaths. After all the names were called to represent the nation's officers with that rose, Zechariah would be called.

Hearing his name called on the lawn of the US Capitol, "Zechariah Cartledge from Running 4 Heroes will be placing the rose to honor all of our nation's fallen heroes…"—that was a surreal moment. They don't invite just anybody to do that. They said they asked Zechariah because they knew every family placing a rose on that same wreath was a family his efforts impacted. They knew having him do that would mean a lot for those surviving families.

That was indeed an honor that we will never take for granted. We thank the Law Enforcement Memorial Fund and the National Fraternal Order of Police for making that possible and including Zechariah in something personal.

It was the hottest day that day. The sun cooked us; we didn't have any sunscreen. We ended up canceling our plans that night because I was burnt to a crisp and had sun poisoning. It was so hot, but would we do it again? Absolutely. It was such an honor to represent all of our nation's fallen heroes.

It indicated how much of an impact one kid has made, starting with a single mile around his neighborhood.

In Closing

It all started with a kid and a chance meeting with the widow of an officer lost on 9/11. What then inspired a one-mile run has led to an organization that has raised almost a million dollars for first responders, surviving families, and canines and conducted over 1,800 miles for those fallen heroes. It has also inspired other kids nationwide to pick up that flag and run a mile to honor these heroes.

Despite the many challenges of leading a national non-profit, the core of what we created is a platform to honor those heroes who make the ultimate sacrifice. This mission means so much to so many. I will continue to do everything I can to support the vision that first came from that little child back in 2018 – a vision to ensure that the memories of the fallen last for eternity and that the Lord is blessed through the actions we make to honor our fallen heroes… one mile at a time.

"…and a little child shall lead them."

Isaiah 11:6 NKJV

Chapter 22

From the Co-Author

Co-authoring this book with Chad is more than an honor. When I contacted him on Facebook, I told him I'd like to write Zechariah's story if he didn't already have someone in mind. Chad had the beginnings of a first chapter when he planned to write the story, but with his responsibilities and traveling, he didn't have the time to write and complete a book.

This is where God had already orchestrated what Chad and I thought was *our* idea. Chad and I share our Christian faith, and we understand that when God places His plans in our hearts and minds, He will reveal them to us in His perfect timing.

My Reason, My Son

My son is a police officer in Chattanooga, TN, and I have always supported law enforcement, so my heart bleeds blue. In my late 20s, I filled out an application with my local police department, coming close to choosing that career path, but God knew the plans He had for me – not to be an officer, but to *raise* one.

I'm a police mom, and to be a police mom, you become a mom to all the men and women who serve in law enforcement. You pray for and support all of them as if they were yours. Our son, Andrew, followed *Running 4 Heroes* from the start of their mission, and I would see him sharing their posts on Facebook. I was amazed with Zechariah and began following the page, too.

Andrew has a "loyal" gene in his DNA. When he sets his heart toward something, his passion for it is fierce and respectful. I knew he respected this organization and understood Zechariah's passion because he had the same heart as a boy.

Loving My Hero

2020 was stressful for almost everyone, even those whose lives were still running smoothly – the *world* was in chaos. It was as if we were driving on our journeys and listening to our favorite radio station, and the frequency went out, leaving us to change the dial and find something else but to keep going.

Andrew is an Army Veteran who completed an Iraq tour in 2010-2011, "Operation Iraqi Freedom." His experience was something only other veterans would understand. As an Army mom, I tried to understand what I could and would always support him. After his return, I understood there would be emotions from things he saw and would deal with occasionally, and he had to find a new normal in a civilian world.

God created my son to be a soldier—and an officer. Whatever it took in his personality to do his job, I didn't question, though it was heartwrenching when I saw him closing off. Moms know when their child has an *unsettling* in their heart, but this is where we must fully trust God to equip our heroes, and we do the fighting with them—but on our knees.

Andrew lives four hours away from us. We have several animals to care for, as does Andrew's family, so visiting and coordinating animal care and everyone's schedules make it difficult to visit often. As a mom, I depend on those texts or calls to stay in communication with our son.

Andrew became a police officer in 2017. When the 2020 pandemic hit, I didn't hear from Andrew as much as I wanted. It was a dark time for LEOs, as much anti-police rhetoric was spewed across the media. I looked for ways to give my love to him while the whole world was transitioning and shifting.

In August of 2022, when Chad and I began our book journey, it was another way for me to show love to Andrew and that I supported him. Any time I supported law enforcement— I was *loving my son.* After the pandemic, when rioting was happening across our nation, I went to my local police department, knelt at the bench outside their doors, and prayed for our police officers. I did this several times. Though Andrew would never know that I was loving *him* through my support for law enforcement— God knew, and He would give that love to Andrew somehow.

The Book

When Chad and I started this book, I got a glimpse of what he sees daily. We met each Wednesday morning on Zoom, and he told me his story chapter by chapter. We recorded it, and I would transcribe each session into notes and format the story onto the manuscript, but this is Chad's story —a father's story about his son's enormous heart and how Zechariah made a difference in the world.

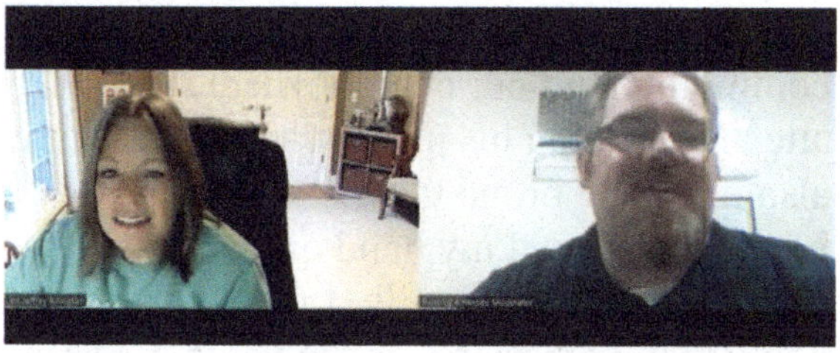

I was so touched throughout writing his story. I cried, laughed, and knew this story needed to be heard.

Meeting at the 2022 Gala

I met Chad and his family in person a few months after we began this book. My husband Jason and I would later attend the first Running 4 Heroes Gala and tour the Tribute Hall. I was enthralled by the beauty of the hero displays and felt a deep respect and reverence. My husband and I found the name of a hero from our hometown of Calloway County, Kentucky. Chief Deputy Jody Cash was shot and killed in the line of duty outside the Marshall County Sheriff's Office. His passing left a great void in our community and our church where Jody attended. Seeing his name was surreal, but it also made me proud that he was being honored. I placed my hand over his name and prayed for his family. I was happy to know that Zechariah was the youth who ran the mile for Jody.
https://www.facebook.com/watch/?v=3326940930861206

I spent a little time with Zechariah while he ate pizza with his officer buddies at the R4H Headquarters. It was Zechariah's 14th birthday.

Meeting Zechariah 2022

Jen and Zechariah at the first Blue Tie Gala

Chloë and Susan at the 2022 Gala

Co-Authors Cartledge and Billington

Jen, with husband Jason

While captivated by the weekend celebrations, I wished my LEO son could be there with me. I had asked Zechariah if he would give a shout-out to Andrew and let me take a video. Zechariah was tired and hungry, but he never let that show. He was ready to honor my son without skipping a beat with a "hello" and "thank you for your service" message.

A special message to Officer Andrew Carter, my son...

I told him about Andrew, how he went to Iraq while in the Army, how he was a major UT Vols fan, and his heart for serving. I put Zechariah's video message on YouTube in private mode and sent my son the link. Only he could see the video. *One view* – I knew Andrew had watched it. My heart was full. I changed the privacy settings after I knew he'd seen it. It let me know he was still *in touch* despite not responding to my texts.

With my son living four hours away, We visit as often as possible. I am so proud of him. My part in this book was another way to show love to my LEO through the miles.

Through patience and understanding, I learned to trust that God would care for Andrew's heart and mind for whatever happens when he clams up.

God answered my prayers, Andrew began texting me back, and we'd talk on the phone between my visits. I needed that.

When loving someone in law enforcement, breaking through their walls isn't always easy, but we cannot understand all they go through and what they face daily.

It is so important to support our first responders. They are putting their lives on the line, as not many people would. How can saying thank you ever be enough?

Me and my Bug before going on a ride along.

Me and my son, Corporal Andrew Carter

Clowning with his brothers, Jonathan and Nathan.

Andrew's stepdaughter, Lacey, has joined law enforcement as a police officer. My daughter-in-law Stephanie and I have grown closer through the years because of our fervent prayers for our heroes in blue.

Andrew's stepdaughters, Macey and Lacey, wife Stephanie, and daughter Ellie Cheyenne.

My LEO son

Now that you know Chad's story and a little of mine, we want you to hear stories of a few others whose lives were touched by the Running 4 Heroes organization. The interviews I conducted with these individuals were difficult to hear, but as they shared their stories, it was natural to feel a deep admiration and compassion for them. This allowed us to connect with the remarkable spirits of the heroes we wholeheartedly honor.

Chapter 23

The Heroes' Stories

The men and women who put their lives on the line, whether that line is blue, red, or green—our first responders have a story. To close, we are giving you a few testimonies from those who, Running 4 Heroes, made a difference in their lives. The heroes and the surviving families are what this mission is all about, and we want you to know the impact Running 4 Heroes has made in the world and what it means to families.

Steven A. Carnes
End of Watch 11-13- 22

Criminal Investigator Steven A. Carnes

Tom Green County District Attorney's Office, Texas

Wife, Jodi Carnes

Jodi met her husband, Steven, at the Jaycee's Haunted House in St. Angelo, Texas. She was with her cousin and said, "Let's grab onto the first two guys that don't have dates, and we'll act like we're scared, and they'll be our date for the night."

It wasn't Steven who Jodi grabbed onto, but his best friend, while her cousin held onto Steven. They had dated for about three months until her cousin moved away. Sixteen-year-old Jodi had been dating Steven's friend, David. As that relationship fizzled, Steven swooped in and asked Jodi on a date. The two became inseparable, dating for eight years and then marrying and having a son.

"Steven was the kind of guy that didn't say anything unless he meant it. He didn't become friends with people immediately and didn't trust people until they had proven trustworthy – he was a cop, even before he was a cop," Jodi says. "When you were in his close circle, he felt comfortable enough to let loose, and he could be the funniest guy in the room."

Jodi strongly recalls Steven's integrity. "He's the guy you could rely on to do the right thing. He was there for you. My mother worked, so he took my younger sister to school when she lived outside the school district she wanted to attend. Steven was that kind of guy," Jodi declares.

November 13, 2023

It was 1:30 in the morning when Jodi received a life-changing call. "I had just texted Steven about 12:30 and knew he would be home in about an hour, so I went to sleep. An hour later, I got a call from the ER nurse, but I was asleep and didn't hear it. My son Bradley was still awake, and they had called him. He came into my room and said, 'Mom, the ER is trying to call you; wake up,' as he said that, my phone rang again, and I snapped into action and picked up the phone," Jodi recalls.

The nurse told Jodi her husband was very ill and that she needed to come to the emergency room immediately. Still half asleep, Jodi was dumbfounded, wondering how her husband would be sick when she had just spoken with him, and things were fine. Jodi, a nurse herself, asked, "Can you tell me what is wrong with him?" And the nurse said she could not. "And that's when I knew," Jodi says, "I have been a nurse for 32 years and know that you don't tell devastating news over the phone."

Jodi threw on clothes as quickly as possible and drove with Bradley to the hospital, shaking the whole way, "I had tunnel vision and was speeding – all I could think was that I just had to get there." City police officers who weren't in Steven's department were there but did not speak to Jodi. She went to the desk and told the clerk she needed to see her husband, and they ushered Jodi to a room.

"That was another validation that he was dead," Jodi thought. She kept those thoughts from her son, and as he asked questions, she told him, "Something must have happened. I don't know what's wrong." Jodi and Bradley wait in the room for what seems an eternity. "I was pacing back and forth, feeling like I would vomit. I was mad that they wouldn't let me back there. The nurse who called me eventually came into the room and said they were working on my husband, and I told her I didn't care what was happening – just let me back there. I am a nurse; I have seen it all. And she told me not yet. I said okay," Jodi explained with tears.

Looking for a trash can to throw up in, Jodi had all she could take in that little room. She found a security guard and told him with gritted teeth, "I want to see my husband now – I am done waiting in that little room!"

Shortly after, a nurse and doctor entered the room and asked Jodi to sit. Defiantly, she told them no, yet found herself obliging their request while preparing for what she knew she was about to hear. She needed to be next to her son. The doctor said, "Mrs. Carnes, I'm sorry, but your husband's gone. We did everything we could do."

Nobody had told Jodi what had happened, and she wanted to know. They told her there was a struggle at work when he arrested someone, and Steven suffered a heart attack. The drunken suspect would not allow himself to be handcuffed, and he was a big, tall football player; Steven was an older, overweight cop – it was not a very good match. Steven had already let this young man go home once when he had caused trouble, but he had returned, causing trouble again.

Before Steven attempted the arrest, he had called for officers to do the transport, and they had arrived when Steven got the suspect handcuffed, but as he stood up, he was having difficulty. They called EMS, and they took him to the hospital.

The doctor stated that Steven coded three times in the emergency room. "At that moment, everything just went black," Jodi says, "Brad immediately cried; I was already crying and felt like I couldn't breathe. Somehow, I ended up on the floor and wrapped my arms around Bradley's legs, holding him and laying my head against him."

Before entering the room where her husband lay, Jodi was warned that it wasn't cleaned up yet. Jodi didn't care; she needed to be by Steven's side. "It looked like a tornado had hit the room with the things they used when Steven had coded," Jodi recalls. "His boots were in the corner of the room, which was a powerful image to me," she says, weeping. "Steven's face was purple. Brad and I held his hand, and we prayed. We talked to him and held him for a while," Jodi sobs.

"We were in the room with him for hours. I wasn't leaving; I needed to touch my husband. I needed to kiss him. I needed to kiss his face and his hands – I needed to feel him because I knew I would never touch him again. I even smelled his shirt because that smell would be different after he was at the funeral home. I needed to take him in one last time," Jodi mourns.

Tears emerged from the deep well of her heart and sprung up like a healing fountain, "I told him how much I had enjoyed being his wife and that I didn't deserve it, but I was glad he let me. I don't think I was ever the wife that he was the husband," Jodi concedes. "He was the best part of our marriage and the best part of me." Steven's parents had already passed on, but he had a sister with Traumatic Brain Injury (TBI) for whom he was responsible. Jodi now bears the responsibility and considers it an honor.

Jodi's Connection with R4H

Jodi had not heard of Running 4 Heroes and wouldn't until the department Steven worked for ruled his death as a "line of duty" death. Once a death is declared *in the line of duty*, the Officer Down Memorial Page website will post the officers' photos and information. Running 4 Heroes retrieves their information from this website.

"Because he was working an extra security job and he wasn't on their clock, the department insisted it was not a line of duty death," Jodi says, "although he had their permission, badge, gun, truck, and radio to apprehend the suspect, they fought with me about it being a line of duty death, for months after Steven died. So I had to have TMPA contact them and say, 'Look, he didn't have to be on the clock at all, as long as he was doing something related to law enforcement that was in his scope of practice.' It's line of duty – period," Jodi maintains.

The San Angelo Police Department made Sgt. John Bouligny Jodi's liaison. He said, "I didn't know him at all, but he has turned out to be a dear friend of mine. It took them from November to February to admit that Steven's death was in the line of duty before it would go onto the ODMP website," Jodi says.

Jodi wasn't aware when Running 4 Heroes ran a mile in honor of Steven. "On February 7, 2022, I received a message on Facebook from Katie Jo. She is Anthony's grandmother, and Anthony is the youth runner who ran for Steven." Jodi states. Katie told Jodi about the run and sent her the link to the video. "It was three days before what would have been our 27th wedding anniversary, and I was in a dark place, wondering how I would get through this anniversary without Steven," Jodi expresses.

When she watched the video, she was moved that people who didn't know her husband were willing to honor him in such a beautiful way. It hurt Jodi that the people who knew Steven fought her about making the line-of-duty death official.

"The people who should have been there for me made my life exponentially harder while people hours away from me were willing to honor him so beautifully. I was floored. It saved me at that moment and changed the trajectory of my life. It was so powerful that it left an imprint on my heart. There will never be a time in my life that the video honoring my husband doesn't matter."

Jodi frequently turns to the video when she needs comfort.

Jodi wanted to know more about Running 4 Heroes, and why they would honor her husband, so she researched the web. She found their website and began reading about the organization. She started following them on Facebook and donating to fundraisers. "It made me feel good because I was doing something that helped others to have their heroes honored. I wanted every goal in my life to be in Steven's honor. He was such a beautiful soul who should still be here with us, and I need to keep his memory alive.

When I read how Zechariah had a dream, and his dad supported him, I was touched – every parent wants to help their child, so I understood, but then I saw how quickly it had grown and become so prevalent. Too many parents instruct their kids to be against law enforcement, and it was good to see so many who were not doing that. "I thought, 'Man, this is big; I need to be a part of this'."

Board Member

Jodi wanted to be more involved, so she told her son Brad about the Tribute Hall in Winter Springs and asked if he'd like to see it. She had talked to Chad a few times and asked if he would like to add Steven's things to the Tribute Hall. "Absolutely," Chad told her, and Jodi brought a suitcase full. "For whatever reason, God was telling me to do this," Jodi says, "there was no doubt in my mind."

When they toured the Tribute Hall, Jodi and Bradley were amazed. "It was the most moving thing I had ever been through, and my husband's things weren't even displayed yet, but all the other heroes come alive when you are in there, and you feel their souls," Jodi conveys.

"Now, there is a beautiful tribute to Steven, and many people are learning about him because of Running 4 Heroes. That was my goal – for people to know about Steven," Jodi says. "He lived and breathed being a police officer for 28 years. It was his only love other than me and Brad."

Connecting with Running 4 Heroes came at the right moment. With fighting the agency and her upcoming wedding anniversary, Jodi didn't think her life could worsen. "I'd lost my best friend – the love of my life, and there I was, having to fight for his honor, and then this beautiful thing happened when I needed it most," she says.

Jodi was part of a podcast with a pro-law enforcement agency sharing about Steven. Chad watched it and approached Jodi about becoming a board member for Running 4 Heroes. "Being on the board has helped me continue the healing process. As a widow, one of the best things I can do is be accountable. If I am not accountable to anyone or anything, I would sit around and cry all the time. I am thankful for it; it was all God's plan," she says.

Jodi eventually stepped down from the board but remains involved with Running 4 Heroes and continues to support the mission.

Celebrating Steven

It is Jodi's goal to keep Steven's memory alive and to continue to honor him. "We had a birthday party for Steven's birthday, July 3rd, inviting all of our friends and family, and had a cake for him," she says. "We all talked about him and our memories. We laughed, loved, and did everything you did at a birthday party. I couldn't let his birthday come and go and do nothing," Jodi insists.

On November 4, 2023, a 5k in Steven's honor was held. The proceeds were split between two organizations important to Jodi and her family, Running 4 Heroes and San Angelo Christian Academy - the school Bradley attended from First to 12th Grade. "Steven's *End of Watch* date is a month away, and I have to keep moving forward with Steven in the front," Jodi says, "with his name and memory always in front of me."

Through tears, she says, "I can't let him go and not let others know about him. I want everyone to know him. I am sad they didn't already because they missed out on a great human being."

Grant Recipient, Samantha Hodgson

Shot on December 23, 2019

Born and raised in New York, Samantha Hodgson wanted to be a police officer ever since she was a child. "I was born and raised in New York. I was part of the Girl Scouts, and they brought in a female NYPD officer to one of the meetings. She completely enamored me, and I didn't want to do anything else," Samantha says.

Her grandfather was part of Homeland Security and NYPD, but she didn't find that out until much later. "I was laid-back and calm as a child. I focused on Barbie this, Barbie that," she says. "Then I got into sports - softball and basketball, and I was only five feet tall."

After high school, Samantha briefly joined the United States Air Force, Security Forces, and Military Police. She transitioned out to raise her daughter and now lives in Bryant, Arkansas.

"When my daughter started school, I became a civilian law enforcement officer with Little Rock PD and did 911 dispatching to learn the other side of the radio," Samantha says. She has been with the Bryant PD for five years. "The desire to become an officer clicked when 9/11 happened. I was stationed in Alaska and responded to several suicidal subjects. I wanted to help these people and let them know they have an outlet. If I can be that tool, I want to be that tool forever," Samantha insists.

December 23, 2019, two days before Christmas, Samantha was dispatched to a suicidal call. "It is ingrained in you that no call is routine. Initially, the mom of the assailant didn't give us the right address," Samantha recalls, "but cops are nosey, and we figure stuff out."

It was Samantha's call, and she would oversee how it went down. A new officer to the department (though not to law enforcement) was training with the corporal, and they happened to be on the call.

"I knocked on the door a few times before the man started yelling," Sam remembers. "Doors are the fatal funnel - another ingrained thing - we don't stand in the middle of the doorway; we go to either side."

The person on the inside never opened the door, so Samantha knocked again. "I got called every name I didn't realize I had," she says. "In training, we were taught that sometimes males don't want to talk with female police and would rather interact with a male officer."

The man was interacting with Officer Hastings when Samantha suddenly heard a loud noise and fell backward. "When I opened my eyes, I remember looking at the guys that were with me," Samantha says, "at that moment, I knew what happened - I'd been hit. I dropped a big ol' F-bomb because I didn't know *where* I was hit and didn't know where the assailant was."

Corporal McCabe stood in the stairwell and called out, "Shots fired! Officer down!" - a phrase no officer ever wants to hear or say. Samantha couldn't get up. She only knew she was dragged down two flights of stairs.

"I remember telling the guys, 'I'm okay.' I tried kicking my feet to help them go faster," Sam conveys.

She remembers being taught how to breathe during combative circumstances in combat training. "Slow, steady breaths take your mind off what is happening while focusing on breathing."

Officer Hastings had *quick-clot gauze* and put it on Samantha's neck. He and McCabe drug her a little further out to the parking lot. "I recall being put in the ambulance and giving them my birthday, but when they sat me up, I started to go in and out," Samantha says, "I looked down at my badge and saw blood."

Later, Sam would find out that she had FaceTimed her aunt while in the ambulance, but she didn't remember doing that. "One of the things I needed for healing was to watch my video from the body cam. It turned out that my daughter called me while the guys were dragging me. From what I heard on the body cam, I answered the phone and told her I was okay," Samantha says.

Med-Flight was dispatched, and as Samantha was put on the helicopter, she told the flight nurse, "I know it's getting dark out, but it's getting *really* dark… and I know it's cold out, but I'm *freezing*." She told Samantha that she was okay, and Samantha repeated, "I'm okay."

When being rolled through the hospital, she could feel every bump. Though she wouldn't see out of her left eye for three months, Samantha remembers seeing shadowy figures standing in the hallway. "In my mind, they were guardian angels."

In the trauma room, she told the nurse she needed to go to the bathroom and that she was going to be sick. She threw up and didn't remember much afterward.

Samantha had surgery on her eye and asserts, "The guy used a 12-gauge shotgun with birdshot. I wouldn't be here now if he had used anything different."

Samantha was in the hospital for five days and out of work for nine months. She could have completely retired and done something else, but she knew nothing else fit her. She was meant to be an officer.

A CAT Scan revealed pellets still in her brain. "I cannot have an MRI anymore because four pellets are still in there, and I also set off metal detectors," she says.

Samantha's daughter, Abigail, did not want her to go back to work. Samantha still experienced PTSD triggers whenever she heard helicopters and remembered the moment on Medflight. "I made a deal with Abby that I could be an SRO (School Resource Officer), be on light duty, and make the transition slowly. I did a little light duty, did some street, and became an SRO," Samantha says.

Abigail is now a junior, and her mom works at her school. "I'll be here until she graduates, then return to the streets – I miss it."

Running 4 Heroes Impact

Samantha had seen a few clips about Running 4 Heroes but had gotten to know them much more after her incident. She contacted them because she wanted to help other officers who went through trauma. "I wanted it to help somebody else – for them to know that you can look death in the eye and say, 'No, I've got this; I'm not done yet.'."

Chad called Samantha as she was heading into plastic surgery to have a few pellets removed, and she later called him back. "He thought my story was phenomenal and told me they wanted whatever I could share, and ever since, we have kept in contact. I share about the organization like crazy, telling people about it," Samantha says.

"We had a softball tournament recently, and our chaplain wore a Running 4 Heroes shirt. We took a selfie together, and I sent it to Chad - it was like a full-circle moment," she says.

When Zechariah and his dad went to Bryant, Samantha showed them around. They had dinner and toured the Police Department. "Our chief and everybody were there," Samantha says. Zechariah presented a check to me, and it was initially supposed to be for five thousand, but they surprised me with an extra thousand."

At the time of the shooting, Samantha was in debt. "I was a single mom trying to figure it out. That six thousand paid off credit card debt, paid off Abby's furniture… it was one of those tools that helped me heal. Because of Running 4 Heroes, that stress was taken off, and I could focus on getting back to work and making sure my therapy was going well without worrying about getting caught up," Samantha says, "it took a huge burden off."

She was impressed with how young Zechariah was, his attitude toward others, and his outlook on life. "I was blown away watching him do his runs and the way he talks to everybody - I'm like, 'nope, you can't grow up.'"

When an Alexander officer was killed in the line of duty, Zechariah came out again. "We contacted the Alexander PD, and Zechariah came out here for a mile run," Samantha says. "Many people didn't know what Running 4 Heroes did for me or what they stood for, but the family of the officer killed still has the flag put up nicely in their house. It meant a lot to them."

Still amazed, Samatha says, "The youngest person on the planet has our back! Zechariah is so young, and having that caring outlook is huge. And all the other kids he is influencing is phenomenal."

A lot has changed since the night of the shooting. Samantha must wear braces to realign her jaw, and she still deals with PTSD. "I am still going through things, but EMDR therapy and the tools on how to process everything have helped me work through it," she says. "My trigger is hearing helicopters. I remember blacking out and going into the helicopter. I think I had it programmed in my brain that I *died* in the helicopter."

Samantha wasn't dying but was administered Fentanyl. After six months of healing, she shot a shotgun, and it didn't bother her. Sirens didn't bother her either. She even went back to the apartment complex where she was shot and saw blood stains and a hole in the door.

"What is crazy is I now live in the apartment complex where that happened," Samantha says. "Going home every day was a challenge for a while."

Her assailant had been shot when he came out and aimed his shotgun at one of the officers. Samantha donated her uniform and everything she wore that night, except her badge, to the Running 4 Heroes Tribute Hall. "I will forever wear that badge," Samantha says.

Moving forward, Samantha got married on October 31, 2023.

Her advice to other officers dealing with trauma is to not dwell on the negative. "Work through it, get through it, and you will be on top living life as you imagined you would," she says. "It's not about *the day you got shot* – it's about *the day you're still alive*. You're not done yet."

Chapter 24

Another Father's Heart

Father, Merced Corona

Retired Sheriff's Sergeant with Colusa County, Merced, served 26 years in law enforcement, and the blue ran through his oldest daughter's veins, too. "Natalie was the oldest of our four girls," Merced says, "she was tall for her age (she grew to be about six foot tall) —and always stood out." Natalie loved being outside and playing sports. She boxed for the LA Corona

Boxing Club in Arbuckle, Calif., where her father coached her. Merced continues to run and coach the registered USA Boxing gym. "Natalie was part of the boxing club and had five amateur fights. She was a good fighter because she was tall and had a long reach," Merced says. Natalie's genuine love of sports was basketball and volleyball. She excelled in those sports.

"She always loved law enforcement—she always had excitement," he says. "She took a liking to officers and greeted them whenever she saw them—especially some of my friends who came over to visit after I retired."

As Natalie got to know some of the officers, her dad knew she had the *calling*. "All she wanted to do was talk about it, and I couldn't see her doing anything else." Natalie had learned the numeric alphabet the police use so she could listen to the scanner and know what they were talking about. Merced's brothers would tell her, "Nat, you're so beautiful and tall – you should model…" but Natalie showed no interest. She knew what she wanted. As a young girl, Natalie would be left in charge of her younger siblings, and by the time her parents got home, the house would be cleaned and in order. "She was always very responsible, even as a young kid," says Merced.

The Blue Dress Photo

Natalie was in high school when the iconic photo was taken. She worked at a fruit stand in the City of Williams, about ten miles from their home.

A photographer, Richard Lau, got to know Natalie when he photographed one of the girls who worked at the fruit stand. Lau took many of the high schooler's senior portraits and asked Natalie if she would mind letting him take photos of her. At first, Natalie said, 'No, I'm not pretty enough for that stuff,' but he and Natalie developed a friendship, and Lau convinced her to be one of his test models as he practiced his photography.

"Richard said this pose was all her idea – she knew what she wanted to do," Merced says. It took Natalie a few weeks to find a dress that was the perfect color to match the blue line flag. "She wanted the picture to honor the men and women serving - especially those who have lost their lives," Merced conveys.

"Richard said when she was holding the flag, all of a sudden, this gust of wind just came up and blew that flag perfectly. In one angle, the slit in her dress showed her thigh, and she discussed it with her mom, and her mom said, 'No, no, that is showing too much leg. Use the other one.' Natalie wanted to use the photo to honor the men and women in uniform."

Becoming an Officer

While attending college, Natalie started as a community service officer for the City of Davis through a professor at Woodland Community College and worked there until the funding ran out. "She had two or three jobs at the time, and to find time to manage all this, she asked if she could *volunteer* after funding had run out," Merced says. Natalie worked a year and a half as a volunteer. Merced says, "She couldn't get enough of it – she loved it. When she was going to go to the academy, the sheriff's department was hiring trainees. I still have friends there, and the sheriff is a personal friend. He called me and said he understood Natalie was interested in police work. They had a couple of spots open, so I tried to get her to apply at the sheriff's department, and she said, 'No, I love Davis; that's where I want to work.' She fell in love with the area.

It made us happy, too, because we felt Davis was pretty safe."

Davis is known as a quiet college community. Merced's nephew David tried to get her to apply at California Highway Patrol because he wanted her to get on the highway patrol, but Natalie was insistent that she wanted to stay at Davis Police Department. She attended the academy and completed all 16 weeks of her field training. FTO training ended, and she was on her third week as a solo officer.

"I still remember the day she became a solo officer and completed her training," Merced says, "she had FaceTimed me, and she pointed her camera to the seat next to her and said, 'Look, Dad, do you see anything? What do you see?' And I said, 'Nothing… what am I supposed to be looking for?' She said, 'Exactly, Dad!' She was so happy."

The Shooting

It happened at about 6:43 pm. Natalie worked the night shift, but one of the female officers had just gone on maternity leave, and she moved into that squad to cover for that officer. "That squad was known as 'the go-getters' – it was the squad everyone wanted to be on," says Merced. "When they selected Natalie, she was thrilled and said, 'I'm going to be on Lavi's squad,' Lavi was the sergeant. She wasn't supposed to be working that night, and there was confusion between my wife and me about whether she was working when we heard about the shooting because it was her first day rotating into this squad."

Natalie got to the office and heard a call being dispatched to one of the other officers. It was a *three-car, minor accident.* The ambulance was there, and the fire department closed the area.

"It was a *nothing* call," Merced says, "She told the dispatcher, 'No, tell them I'm going,' the dispatcher said, 'Natalie, are you crazy? It's just a bunch of paperwork. There are no injuries'."

Natalie told the dispatcher to tell the other officer she was en route. She wanted more experience, so she loaded her car and sped off. "That's why… it's an act of God," says Merced, "because so many things happened for her to be there that day; you can't say if this wouldn't have happened or if that… there were too many things that put her there."

The Back Story

The gunman, Kevin Limbaugh, had made calls to the Davis Police Department, reporting that they were harassing him and sending ultra-sonic signals and wouldn't let him sleep. The troubled man had also been fired from his job for assaulting a co-worker. The department believed the lights and sirens triggered his response to the three-car accident, and Limbaugh armed himself and rode his bike around the block, according to the witness standing next to Natalie – the second driver.

"Natalie was taking down her information; the witness had a backpack on – she was a student," Merced says. "They saw him pull up on his bicycle and lay it down, and he leaned on a picket fence. Natalie looked over but thought it was just somebody being a 'lookie-loo,' so she continued writing down the information when they heard the first shot."

In an instant, the gunman pushed off from the fence and broke one of the boards as he aimed. The two ladies turned when they heard the crack of the board break, and Natalie was hit in the neck right above her vest. She immediately went down, and Limbaugh continued to fire at her.

"We don't know how many shots he fired, but there were many rounds in her," Merced says. The student took off running, and the guy turned the gun and shot her in the back. The bullet went into her backpack, through a book and laptop, and it stopped the bullet," Merced says. Officer Natalie Corona was down -the gunman unloaded an entire magazine.

"Three rounds were lethal; the neck, two went in through her side, and one shot went above and sideways across her chest. Then he turned the gun on the fireman about ten feet away. The fireman slipped and fell, and the guy shot until he ran out of bullets. The fireman scrambled around to avoid getting hit and took one round in the boot," Mercede retells.

"When the guy was reloading, the fireman took off running. The gunman shot at anything moving, plus a transit bus, missing a lady by inches. He was shooting at Natalie's car, the fire trucks, and the firefighters who were running away. They could hear the bullets whizzing over their heads. Luckily, no one else was killed that night," he says.

Limbaugh returned to his house, leaving a backpack with his ID at the scene, and police were able to track him to his house immediately. "According to his roommate," Merced conveys, "he was sweating, agitated, and pulled open a beer. The roommate asked what he had done, and he said, 'You need to get out of here; I just did something bad.'"

As police began to surround the house, Limbaugh stepped outside wearing a bulletproof vest. Merced says, "He had armed himself and just waited for the police out on his patio. Once he was surrounded, he went back in and shot himself. He knew he wasn't going anywhere."

Natalie was the first officer with the Davis Police Department to die in the line of duty since 1959.

Hearing the News

Merced recalls receiving the devastating yet surreal news, "We were at a basketball game for my third daughter, Kathy. It would be an excellent game, with our rival school for the championship. We were all there: my wife, three daughters, and myself.

"My phone rang, but I noticed it was from people who usually don't call me, and I thought I'd get it later. Lupe and my daughters started getting calls themselves and spoke to one of our family members saying, 'It sounds like there was a shooting in Davis,' but I said, 'Don't worry about it – we'll look into it after the game ends.'

Merced knew Natalie wouldn't be on duty until later that night. "I said, 'Don't worry— it wasn't Natalie; she's not even working yet.' I think Lupe felt something was not right," he says. More calls kept coming, and Lupe heard the news of a female officer injured, but Merced assured her that Natalie was not working.

Soon after, an officer texted and said *Natalie was involved.* "We didn't know the extent of any injuries; we just knew she was involved in the shooting. They were right in the middle of the game, but we were trying to figure out what to do— we knew we needed to get over there, and we scrambled to get off the bleachers," Merced says.

It was a packed house. The family started out the door when Lupe said, "What about Kathy? She is still playing…" Merced went to the coach and said, "You need to call a timeout; we need to get Kathy. Natalie was involved in an incident, and we *all* need to go." The coach stopped the game, and Kathy came off the court. At this moment, Natalie's father knew in his heart that something was dire as the family started out the door. With tears and emotion, he again relives the moment.

"We had gone about 50 feet or so when we got a call from my brother-in-law, saying *the officer didn't make it*. And so… we already knew," he sobs, "we knew it was Natalie; she had been…" Merced's breath leaves him. The silence says the words he can't get out, "…and the department hadn't called. The news said the officer was taken to UC Davis in Sacramento in about 45 minutes."

Merced composes himself and continues. "It was very foggy that night. Lupe tried to call the department. She talked to the dispatcher, who said, 'Let me have the chief call you.' So the chief called. I remember thinking as I was driving that I had laid to rest two of my good academy friends killed in the line of duty. Is this really happening? I laid two of my best mates down, and now my daughter— it was a big blur after that."

The chief informed Merced that they had locked down the city, saying, "Nothing is moving in Davis that we don't know about. We have thousands of officers from all over the place. We'll catch this guy."

Merced tried to merge *life as he knew it* and reality together, trying to make sense of it all, but the information came slowly, and so did processing this trauma as it unfolded. "We started receiving calls from family members who wanted to come over and be with us," he says. News media trucks were outside and wanted to talk to somebody in the family. "I told Lupe I needed to speak to these people; they need their story, and then they can give us our space," Merced contends.

"We brought in two or three at a time. I said, 'You get 15 minutes. You can look at her pictures, and I'll talk to you guys with the promise that you'll give us our space when you get your story'."

Lupe had made a collage of Natalie's photos throughout her school years. The reporters were accepting and understanding.

Their fifteen minutes ended up going into two to three hours. The shooting had affected the whole community.

Merced retired from law enforcement back in 2012. He was a sergeant for 17 years before running for Sheriff and is now a board supervisor for the County. "I got a rocky start on my political career, but it's been good. I just got re-elected, so I'm in the process of serving my second term. We are blessed with a large family and many friends. Natalie's mother,

Lupe, taught school for 30 years, and Merced was in law enforcement for 26 years. The family is active in their church, loved, and surrounded by great support.

Zechariah and the R4H Impact

They found out about Zechariah's run in honor of Natalie about a week or two afterward. "Somebody had seen it on social media somewhere and asked if we had heard about the kid in Florida who ran a mile for her. I can't remember who told us that, but I remember thinking, 'How would they even know about Natalie?' I didn't realize the news had gone national —and even international, because we later got mail from Europe, Mexico, and all these other countries," Merced marvels.

"It touched our hearts because someone cared enough to do something in honor of Natalie and didn't even know her. I told Lupe, 'Can you believe that? Some ten-year-old in Florida ran a mile in her honor,' —she was like, *wow*, we were just in awe." The first time the family met Chad and Zechariah was when Zechariah would present a check to an injured officer in Union City. "Most kids at ten years old don't think about that stuff, and we wanted to be a part of that since they were coming to the area, and after what they had done in honor of Natalie – we were very thankful," Merced says. "We didn't know that Natalie was his first mile that began Running 4 Heroes. When we met them, we discovered that she inspired him to run that first mile."

A local business wanted to honor Natalie with a mural on the outside wall of their business. Merced thought the townspeople might not like it because park benches were already named in her honor. "We had many things going on at that time, and we were sensitive to the fact that others had died and they didn't do anything like that, so at first we told them no," he declared. They were told the artist, Shane Grammar, was well-known and would do an excellent job.

"We discussed it and finally decided it was okay if they wanted to do that. It took about a week to finish and was very beautiful," Merced says.

Chad had asked if the family would mind sharing anything special or memorable of Natalie for the Tribute Hall. Since Natalie had just started, she only had three uniforms. "My wife was very protective because we don't have a lot of that stuff, but as we talked, I said, 'this is going to be like a museum, and it would be a piece people will see rather than the uniforms being in the closet,' so we decided to give one of the shirts," he says, "we wanted it to be special, and we felt *the cause* – that it was worthy of it."

The Tribute Hall Display

When Merced saw the display, it was everything and more than he expected. "I thought they did a fabulous job in the display for Natalie," he says. We felt honored that we could be a part of it."

The Corona family are humble people. They did not seek attention from the tragedy but have found a platform to honor their daughter as well as to support the surviving families of those who were injured or killed in the line of duty and to continue to support these men and women putting their lives on the line.

Respectfully, Merced says, "We have such gratitude for people like Zechariah, Chad, and his family to do this for officers and their families. It will keep our children's memory alive for many years."

The Corona family uses any opportunity to bring awareness of the fact that we lose countless officers yearly. When

Merced speaks at different functions, he wants to bring attention to the fact that our officers are being ambushed, shot, and killed. "It's not going to stop —this is going to continue. It's how society *is* now, and some are against law enforcement, but at least we can honor those officers who have paid that ultimate sacrifice," He says.

Merced understands that officers will continue to risk their lives patrolling and responding to calls with unforeseen danger. "They run *to* fire while everybody else is running *away* from it. I want to do my part in honoring those men and women – even the ones who are still out there, not just the ones killed," Merced insists.

" As long as I live, I want to honor those men and women willing to serve. It sounds cliché, but nothing else matters if we don't have security, and we need to be *thankful* for those men and women serving day and night," he says.

"Whether rain or shine, holidays or weekends, when I speak, I want to be grateful, speak up for those who can't speak, and thank them for their service."

Merced has met several surviving families and understands their agony. "It's so tough. You know the pain they are going through. You've been there and know the long journey ahead of them."

January 2024 will be five years since the fatal shooting. There will be a public ceremony at the Davis Police Department.

"I would tell those surviving families to have faith that their loved ones will *not* be forgotten and that God's hand is in everything — especially in calling them home. They died for a reason, and it is honorable." Merced closes with this assurance, "Your loved one will not be forgotten. Whenever we go to these functions, we still hear about Natalie. They know her story, and it just warms our hearts. People will look at Natalie's display and think, 'Wow, let me read about this officer,' they will learn about her, and she will never be forgotten."

Lupe, Natalie, and Merced Corona

Officer Corona's display at the Tribute Hall

Police Officer Natalie Becky Corona

Davis Police Department, California End of Watch Thursday, January 10, 2019

Chapter 25

Zechariah Speaks

My Passion

I was intrigued by running in first grade. I've played soccer since I was five, always running and active. When I saw a flyer in my elementary school for cross country, I wanted to try out, and I made the team. Distance running was what I did best, and I was among the top three in my county. Then, I started doing 5ks in my community.

With the Tunnel to Towers organization, I was inspired by firefighters and police officers who turned out and ran in their full gear. After that event, I wanted to learn more about who they were. I studied about 9/11 after that because that is what started their organization, and I began raising money for them. We had so much support that I eventually wanted to start Running 4 Heroes. Running was something I was good at, and I wanted to use it for a purpose.

Once I received Walwyn Stuart's name badge at the Tunnel to Towers 5k, I was intrigued to look up his story. Like the other first responders, he was dedicated to serving and left a family behind. He had gone to the south tower and gave his life helping others.

Though I was raising money for the Tunnel to Towers foundation, all the 5k's I ran were for *him*, and I wore his name badge on every run. Dad would record the runs and post them on social media. As I raised money for them that year, Tunnel to Towers invited me to New York City and surprised me and my family by meeting Thelma, the widow of Walwyn Stuart. That was the first time I met a family member of a first responder I ran for. That experience made me want to continue running for first responders.

Walwyn Stuart was the biggest inspiration behind this. That's when I realized –wow, officers and firefighters give so much, and I want to help out more. I was shocked by the number of lives lost.

In my early videos, I would say a prayer for the first responder's families and talk about the tragedy. That's why I'd give a longer speech at the end of the run. I wanted people to realize that with the gun violence officers face or the training and structure fires for firefighters, they are very difficult but important jobs.

We want to spread awareness – so *thank* a first responder when you see one and support their efforts and sacrifice. Running 4 Heroes wants to provide the needs necessary for them and their families if they are injured or killed in the line of duty.

Support

A few people approached me and asked why I was supporting the police (especially during 2020 when everything was going on), and I'd tell them we were running for the first responders who gave their *lives* and made the ultimate sacrifice. I'm not saying *every* first responder has the best mindset, but I believe 99% of first responders who come into their profession genuinely do it to help others.

The few 'bad apples' you hear about are often pushed through the media, so Running 4 Heroes is a way to make others aware of the sacrifices made when a first responder loses their life.

My school was very supportive. I have always been a social person, involved in soccer, cross country, and after-school activities such as Youth Night, so I have an outgoing personality and get along with people. Many people approach me and ask how *they* can start something like I did.

Challenges

As a kid, getting used to running almost every night was a task, especially during the pandemic and before we added the other youth runners. It was a lot to carry for me and my family. The traveling was nearly every week. I was big into aviation then, so I loved flying. Even with all the challenges, it never really affected me negatively. It has always had a positive impact – I had a positive mindset on how everything was going. And even though I was stressed at times, I didn't let it get to me because I knew what we were doing was making a big difference.

Family

My dad has been the biggest help since the beginning - managing and moderating the Running 4 Heroes Facebook page. He is the CEO of our organization, so he has had to undergo all the stress behind the operation. I often heard him up at 4 a.m. still working because it takes that much effort. He has always been there for me and for the organization. That's why we are still moving forward today.

My dad's support– and even my mom and sister's, made a big difference for me. They never skipped a night. They were there 100%. Dad organized everything, my mom took pictures, and Chloë would run with me. It was a team effort, for sure. And it's not just them, but my whole family is supportive. My grandpa came out to every single run before his recent injury caused him to move into an assisted living facility. I can't remember one time when he wasn't there – about 1,400 of the miles I ran. My grandma has always reached out to families of the first responders I ran for, and several of them are friends with her. They talk every day. My whole family has been supportive throughout the years.

Emotionally

Many runs affected me emotionally. None of them are easy or without my heart going into it, but one that stands out was running for honorary Officer Abigail Arias – the seven-year-old girl who lost her battle with cancer. I cried during that run.

There were also many local runs where I teared up. There would be a big turnout of support for the family of the fallen first responder – those are always harder miles. I met one officer from Iowa a week before an incident he was in. I got to know him for about three hours when he led us to our hotel and ate dinner with us. A week later, he was shot seven times and was in critical condition. He did not pass away, so that was a run we didn't have to do – and that was great. We were able to go back to Iowa not long after the incident and present him with an Injured First Responder Grant.

We sadly had two grant recipients we ran for who passed away due to their injuries. One was a deputy from Minnesota, and the other was a firefighter in Texas. I was very emotional during those runs.

Retirement

When I retire at the end of 2024, I will miss running and meeting the families I run for. I'll also miss traveling and the experiences, but I will still be involved. I will find joy in watching the other youth runners honor our fallen with these miles, meeting surviving families, and seeing the organization grow.

When I am eighteen, I can be the CEO, but I honestly don't think I want to be in that role as I see how much work goes into it. As the founder, however, I will definitely remain involved, and I plan to be on the board starting in 2025.

Message to Youth Runners

Though it didn't happen to me personally, because of the sensitive topic of running for fallen police officers and firefighters, I encourage the youth runners not to let *haters* get to them. Don't let others tell you that you are in the wrong seat or have the wrong initiative. I'm sure there are differences in support from other communities. Just keep going – you're doing the right thing and helping many families heal. Also, let somebody know if it's getting to be too much.

I had moments during the pandemic when I ran so much that I felt a lot of pressure. I was so concerned a family might not have a run done for their hero if I took time off, but sometimes you must. And do what you love. Stay with it and continue to help others.

Hobbies

I'm big into SIM and stock car racing, and I also like game design. I freelance for a site called Roblox for various games and projects. I also do a lot of commission freelance work. As a hobby, I'd like to do some part-time racing. I just got a full SIM setup to start racing in more leagues. I'm big into I-Racing.

Thoughts on the Future

I want to attend a college that offers game design programs or teaches social media management. I'm only fifteen right now, so I have a lot of different interests and options ahead of me. I may have to start out at a '9-5,' but eventually, I want to work for myself, and I think I will work better that way. Some people assumed I'd like to be a police officer or firefighter when I grew up. For a while, I considered aviation as a career but changed my mind about flying commercially.

I wouldn't mind having a license to fly a Cessna as a hobby, but a neighbor who is a commercial pilot with a wife and daughter was sometimes gone six days out of the week. He was hopping around the country and living in hotel rooms every night. I realized he didn't have much time to enjoy with his family, and when I grow up, I will want to spend time with my family, and I can do that best if I work for myself.

Epilogue

2024 and Beyond

What makes this mission so special is the youth who lead it. Over the last five to six years, the nation has watched Zechariah grow from a youth runner to a young adult. When he runs now, he has a little bit of a mustache, and his voice is deeper. The country has seen him grow up before their eyes. His impact has made other youths want to carry that flag and banner even after he is through.

As a board, we decided the best age to graduate from the Youth Runner program was when they turned sixteen. Zechariah turns sixteen in 2024. His last mile is scheduled for December 30th, 2024. We anticipate many surviving families, agencies, and folks nationwide for that run.

That particular run will be special because he'll run in honor of every fallen first responder—over 1,500 heroes he ran for. We will do something similar with other youth runners who have been with us for a long time.

A lot is going on for 2024 for various reasons. Not only will Zechariah graduate from the Youth Runner program, but we have outgrown our Tribute Hall. We've moved into a larger facility; it will allow us to tell more of these stories and be more cost-effective for the mission, which is a great thing, but it does require a build-out. So, that being said, 2024 is a big transition year for us.

Running 4 Heroes was about a kid who wanted to do something good, and now it's about multiple kids honoring the lives of the heroes lost. More lives are impacted, more heroes are honored, and it's a culmination of how much this mission has grown.

We hope to open the new Tribute Hall by early 2025. As we undergo these changes, I hope it shows people how one child can impact the lives of others and how much of a difference one individual can make in the world.

Chad Cartledge

Photo Gallery

Little Champ

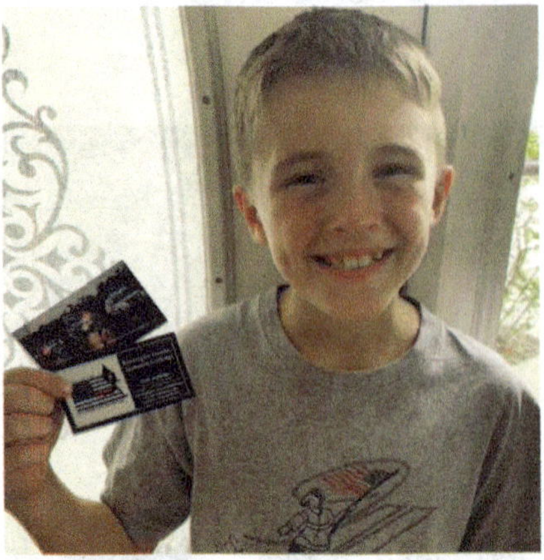

Humble Beginnings

Boy with a Mission

A Fox 35 Interview

Never forgetting Conner

Honorable calling - but not easy

A somber moment

A kiss for his sister - one of his biggest supporters.

"I am my beloved's, and my beloved is mine."

Napping with Schroeder

THIS is how you eat a cheese stick

Father's Day with James Cartledge and Curtis Kaslewicz.

Grandma Susan Wiseman-Gremmel and Curtis Gremmel.

Grams Ellen Kaslewicz

An opportunity to educate students about the events of 9/11 and the Freedom Flag Foundation.

Traditional Father/Son Sunday

Chad and his wife Susan, 2023 Gala

The Cartledges - 2023 Blue Tie Gala

Co-Author Bio – Chad Cartledge

An Orlando native, Chad Cartledge is a proud Christian, husband to his wife Susan, father to Conner, Zechariah, and Chloë, and is a son and brother.

Chad received his Bachelor of Arts in Radio/Television and a Minor in Theater from the University of Central Florida. However, he has spent most of his career in the financial world. Having spent 12 years at Full Sail University in their Financial Aid Department, Chad has been the Full-Time CEO of Running 4 Heroes since January 2022.

When not working on the mission, Chad enjoys time with his family, building LEGO sets, and singing whenever the opportunity allows. This book marks his first experience in writing, and he is honored to share the story of the mission from his eyes with those who have supported the Running 4 Heroes mission.

Co-Author Bio – Jen Jeffrey Billington

Jen Jeffrey Billington is the author of

- *BREADCRUMBS – Finding True Love's Trail,*
- *Faith Blossoms – A Collection of Poems,*
- *12 Doors – A Guide to Kingdom Living,*
- *My Kentucky Birds*
- *Birds, Birds, Birds*
- *Pendom Living,* a children's book series focused on those with special needs.

Jen began her writing career in 2011 while living in New York and later moved back to Chattanooga. She continued her weekly column for the Chattanoogan.com online news publication and other assignments. She also wrote for CityScope magazine. After marrying and moving to her birthplace of Kentucky, Jen published an online magazine called The Murray Mirror for her community. She also wrote for Vue Magazine in Paducah, KY.

Jen resides in Kentucky with her husband, Jason. She is the mother of twin sons who are businessmen and live in Kentucky, and a younger son who is a police officer in Chattanooga. She is also a grandmother to five grandchildren. She enjoys her horse and animals, kayaking, bicycling, and hiking.

For more information about **Running 4 Heroes Inc.**, or to give a donation, please visit the website:

https://running4heroes.org/

To give a donation to **Running 4 Heroes,**
you can go directly to the website by
scanning this QR code.
Thank you!

Made in the USA
Monee, IL
03 November 2026

67384319R00184